I0411446

United States
Department of
Agriculture

Forest Service

Pacific Northwest
Research Station

Resource Bulletin
PNW-RB-245
February 2005

Oak Woodlands and Other Hardwood Forests of California, 1990s

K.L. Waddell and T.M. Barrett

Authors

K.L. Waddell and **T.M. Barrett** are research foresters, Forestry Sciences Laboratory, P.O. Box 3890, Portland, OR 97208-3890.

Photo Credit

Cover photo by Dale Waddell

Abstract

Waddell, K.L.; Barrett, T.M. 2005. Oak woodlands and other hardwood forests of California, 1990s. PNW-RB-245. Portland, OR: U.S. Department of Agriculture, Forest Service, Pacific Northwest Research Station. 94 p.

This report provides a multiownership assessment of oak woodlands and other hardwood forests in California, excluding only reserved lands outside of national forests. Because sampling intensity on woodlands was doubled from the previous 1981-84 inventory, and because national forests were inventoried, this is the most complete assessment to date for California hardwoods. Tables provide estimates for hardwood forest type area, hardwood volume, biomass, numbers of trees, change in forest area, growth, harvest, and mortality. The dates of the inventories used in the assessment, 1991-94 for unreserved lands outside national forests and 1994-2000 for national forests, also allowed an assessment of pre-epidemic conditions for susceptible tree species and forests in a 12-county area affected by sudden oak death.

Summary [1]

For the 1990s, hardwood forests were estimated to cover more than 11.3 million acres (±2 percent sampling error [se; see glossary for definition]), which was 40 percent of forest land in California. Hardwood forest area included 6.7 million acres of oak woodland, 76 percent of which was privately owned, and 0.5 million acres of non-oak woodland. Of the 4.1 million acres of hardwood timberland forest, oak forest types constituted 53 percent.

Blue oak woodland was the most common hardwood forest type in California. Low levels of blue oak regeneration observed in the 1980s continued into the 1990s. In descending order of occurrence, other common hardwood forest types included canyon live oak, California black oak, tanoak, interior live oak, coast live oak, Oregon white oak, and Pacific madrone. Other forest types, including California laurel, Engelmann oak, and valley oak, were uncommon, estimated to be 2 percent or less of the total hardwood forest area in California.

The net growing-stock volume of hardwood tree species on the inventoried area was estimated as 4.7 billion cubic feet (±5 percent se) on woodland and 9.4 billion cubic feet (±3 percent se) on timberland, with California black oak having

---

[1] All estimates exclude reserved land outside of national forests, such as national and state parks. These lands are excluded because they were not inventoried. Estimates of change from the 1980s to the 1990s also exclude national forest land.

the largest growing-stock volume of any hardwood species. The aboveground biomass of hardwood trees on forest land was estimated as 555 million tons (±2 percent se), or 29 percent of overall tree biomass in California forest lands. Combining inventory estimates with other published data indicated that about 2 percent of the estimated board-foot volume in harvested hardwood sawtimber-sized trees went to California sawmills.

An estimated 60,000 acres per decade of hardwood forest was converted to developed land or roads between 1984 and 1994 (upper 68 percent confidence interval is 130,000 acres per decade). Of the common forest types, California black oak had the greatest percentage decrease in area from 1984 to 1994; excluding salvage logging, 11 percent of the black oak forest type on timberland had some black oak trees harvested or cut and left on the plot between 1981-84 and 1991-94. However, overall net growing-stock volume increased for California black oak and other common hardwood species.

Within the 12 counties quarantined as of summer 2004 for *Phytophthora ramorum*, the pathogen associated with sudden oak death, an estimated 3.8 million acres (±4 percent se) of forest land is dominated by the regulated host species of tanoak, coastal redwood, Douglas-fir, coast live oak, California black oak, Pacific madrone, California buckeye, canyon live oak, California laurel, and bigleaf maple. Tanoak, California black oak, coast live oak, and Shreve's oak are tree species that can suffer trunk lesions and associated mortality from *Phytophthora ramorum*. These trees are important to wildlife diversity, contributing to habitat and providing a source of acorns. Although essential characteristics of the disease are still unknown, there appears to be a potential for very extensive changes of forest structure and composition over a geographic range encompassing millions of acres of California forest land, with the potential for many indirect ecosystem effects.

Contents

List of Tables

Introduction

Hardwood forests cover more than 11 million acres of land in California and provide many benefits, including wildlife habitat and food, lumber and other forest products, grazing, watershed protection, open space for recreation, fuelwood, and biodiversity. Hardwood species in California are diverse, including species found throughout western North America, such as quaking aspen (*Populus tremuloides*), and others that are primarily found in California, such as blue oak (*Quercus douglasii*), valley oak (*Quercus lobata*), coast live oak (*Quercus agrifolia*), and interior live oak (*Quercus wislizeni*) (see app. 1 for a list of species names). For many residents, oak woodlands and savannas define the California landscape (fig. 1).

Hardwood forests have been a subject of public focus for many years. Land conversions and clearing have been areas of concern, with conversion to agricultural uses predominant in the first part of the 20th century, and increasing concern over conversion to residential uses and vineyards in more recent years. In 1993, California counties with oak woodlands were directed by the State Board of Forestry to develop oak conservation plans, and most now have mitigation policies or permitting processes for oak removal (Light and Pedroni 2002). Slow regeneration of some species also has been a source of concern. The concern is not new; nearly a century ago a survey of Pacific slope trees noted sparse regeneration for valley oak, Oregon white oak (*Quercus garryana*), canyon live oak (*Quercus chrysolepis*), coast live oak, and blue oak (Sudworth 1908).

Concern for California hardwoods, and oak woodlands in particular, has generated a very active research and education program. Since 1979, five symposia on California hardwoods and oak woodlands have been held (Pillsbury and others 1997, Plumb 1980, Plumb and Pillsbury 1987, Standiford 1991, Standiford and others 2002). The University of California, together with the California Department of Forestry and Fire Protection (CDF), the State Board of Forestry, and the California Department of Fish and Game, established an intensive research and extension program, the Integrated Hardwood Range Management Program (IHRMP), in 1986. A number of nonprofit organizations, such as the California Oak Foundation, also focus on oak and hardwood issues.

In the last few years, sudden oak death has overtaken other issues as a threat to California hardwood forests. Sudden oak death, associated with the pathogen *Phytophthora ramorum*, was first described in 1995 in tanoak (*Lithocarpus*

Figure 1—Oak woodlands characterize large areas of the California landscape.

densiflorus). Subsequently *P. ramorum* was found to affect coast live oak, California black oak (*Quercus kelloggii*), Pacific madrone (*Arbutus menziesii*), bigleaf maple (*Acer macrophyllum*), California laurel (*Umbellularia californica*), and other species (fig. 2). Because of the relatively rapid spread and increased mortality rate for some common species, the disease can be expected to have a substantial effect on many of the hardwood and coniferous forests described in this report. The dates of the inventories used in this assessment, 1991-94 for lands outside national forests and 1994-2000 for national forests, allow the use of these data to provide a pre-epidemic baseline for future monitoring.

Inventories Used in This Report

The USDA Forest Service forest inventory program, called Forest Inventory and Analysis (FIA), inventories forest land, often dividing it into different categories such as timberland and unproductive forest, which includes woodland. Definitions of these and other terms are provided in the glossary. Until the 1980s, statewide forest inventories in California sampled only timberland. In response to increased interest in woodlands, the first statewide inventory of California woodlands and other unproductive forest was made in 1981-84 with results reported as part of an assessment of California hardwoods (Bolsinger 1988).

Figure 2—California laurel leaves infected by *P. ramorum* Sonoma County, 2002.

In 1991-94, a new statewide inventory of woodland was conducted, remeasuring the plots used in the 1981-84 FIA inventory and also doubling the number of plots with tree measurements. Timberland was also inventoried in 1991-94, with a sampling intensity of twice that used for woodland. Neither the 1981-84 nor the 1991-94 inventory included national forests, which contain 21 percent of the unreserved forest land in California. However, during 1994-2000, a comprehensive forest inventory of California national forests was conducted by the National Forest System (NFS).

This report is based on data from these combined inventories: the 1991-94 FIA inventory of timberland, the 1991-94 FIA inventory of woodland, and 1994-2000 NFS inventories of national forests. Because of the inclusion of inventory data for national forests and the increased number of samples for private and other public land, these are the best estimates for California hardwoods that have been made to date. Estimates often differ from those in the report by Bolsinger (1988). These differences are caused by the additional data collected and by changes in estimation procedures and do not necessarily reflect actual changes in hardwood forests. A more limited set of information has been used to estimate change. It is very important to understand the limitations of the inventories and to use the sampling errors that are provided to interpret the information in this report. Greater detail on inventory methods is provided in appendix 2.

Tables of forest estimates are in a separate section at the end of the report. Estimates are given for forest area (tables 1 and 2), volume (tables 3 through 6 and 10), biomass (tables 7 through 9), change (tables 11 through 16), and a few additional attributes. Estimates do not include savannas (land with less than 10 percent tree cover) or land that is devoted to nonforest uses (such as golf courses or city parks). Grazing is considered a forest use in California, and estimates include grazed forest land, although improved pasture land is excluded. Reserved land outside of national forests (primarily state and national parks) has not been inventoried, and it is excluded from all estimates except where noted (fig. 3).

Hardwood Forest Types in the 1990s

Excluding reserved lands outside of national forests, the total estimated area of hardwood forest types in California was 11.29 million acres (±1.7 percent sampling error [se; see glossary for definitions]). Hardwood forest types made up 40 percent of all forest land in California. This included 4.07 million acres (±3 percent se) classified as hardwood timberland and 7.22 million acres (±2 percent se) classified as hardwood woodland and other unproductive forest (table 1). Most hardwood forest was privately owned (70 percent), with a substantial portion in national forest ownership (25 percent) and a relatively small portion in other public ownership (5 percent).

By order of frequency, the most common hardwood forest types were blue oak, canyon live oak, California black oak, tanoak, interior live oak, coast live oak, Oregon white oak, and Pacific madrone. Other hardwood forest types (valley oak, Engelmann oak, California laurel, buckeye, and many others) were relatively uncommon, estimated at 150,000 or fewer acres each (table 2).

California oak woodlands–forest dominated by trees from the genus *Quercus* and not productive enough to be considered timberland–covered 6.7 million acres (±4 percent se). Private ownership accounted for 76 percent of this area, with smaller portions in national forest ownership (18 percent), and other public ownership (6 percent). Oak savannas, with less than 10 percent tree cover, also covered large land areas, although the exact area is unknown. Bolsinger (1988) gave an approximation that 1.8 million acres of land in California is savanna characterized by hardwood trees in grassland, and 1.8 million acres is characterized by hardwood trees in chaparral. A chaparral inventory of 14 counties in the central and southern coast of California estimated that substantial portions of chaparral contain hardwood tree species, including many in the *Quercus* genus (Fried and others 2004).

Hardwood forest types make up 40 percent of California's forest land, of which 70 percent is privately owned.

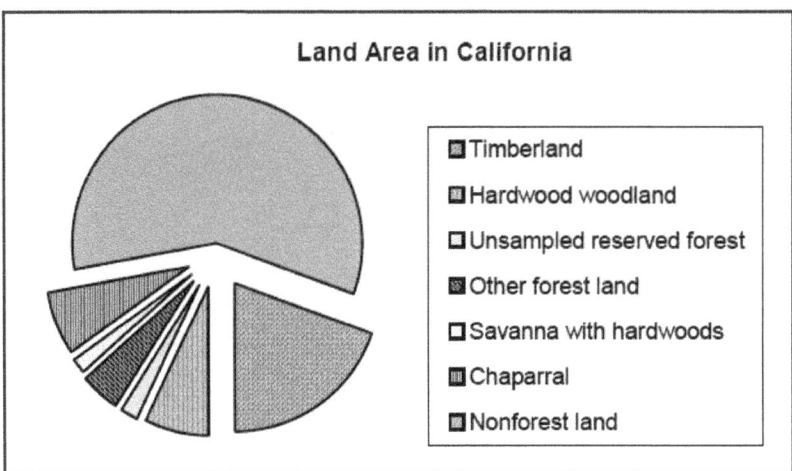

Figure 3—Distribution of land in California.

Some of the oak species hybridize and have overlapping ranges, and forest typing classifies what is often a gradation of mixed species into discrete classes. The classification process for this assessment is based on the concept of predominance of live tree cover for that species, and it is the same classification method that has been used in other Forest Inventory and Analysis reports developed from the 1991-94 data (for example, Waddell and Bassett 1996, 1997a, 1997b). In the 1980s assessment, classification was derived from the predominance by basal area for that species (Bolsinger 1988). Individual trees of a particular species were also found in other forest types. In the following sections, estimates are provided for area where a tree species occurred, as well as area for the forest type where that species was predominant.

Blue oak was the most common hardwood forest type in California in the 1990s.

Blue Oak Forest Type

The most common inventoried hardwood forest type in California was blue oak, with an estimated 3.03 million acres (±5 percent se). As was done in the Bolsinger (1988) report, forest initially classified as ghost pine (*Pinus sabiniana*) was included in the estimate for the blue oak forest type, accounting for 0.11 million acres of the total blue oak forest type. The blue oak forest type occurred in foothill woodlands on all sides of the central California valley with blue oak trees having an extremely similar distribution (fig. 4). This forest type was 90 percent privately owned, with 4 percent on national forest land and 6 percent on other public land. The average elevation for the blue oak forest type was 1,640 feet, with two-thirds of this forest type occurring between 680 and 2,680 feet. Blue oak forest had the lowest average annual precipitation of any of the common forest types, with a

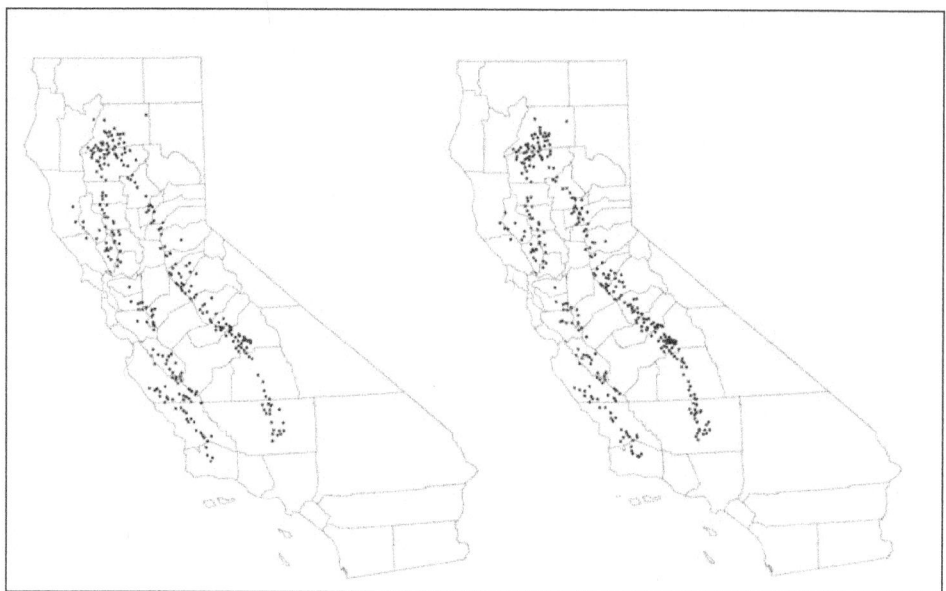

Figure 4—Sample plot locations for the blue oak (*Quercus douglasii*) forest type (left) and for blue oak trees (right). Figure includes plots for all inventories used in this report, and the plots shown did not all have the same probability of selection. To protect landowner privacy, each plot shown has some deliberate location error.

median precipitation of 21 inches per year and two-thirds of the forest type having precipitation between 19 and 25 inches per year.

Although climate is an important factor in explaining the distribution of the blue oak forest type, it is believed that many factors have influenced the present composition and stand structure of blue oak woodlands. Acorn production can be influenced by rainfall and temperature (Koenig and others 1999), but recruitment from acorns and survival can be affected by predation from insects, rodents, deer, and cattle (Adams and McDougald 1995, Borchert and others 1989, Hall and others 1992). Survival of seedlings and saplings appears to be related to both competition and facilitation (for example, shade) from other plants (Standiford and others 1997, Swiecki and others 1997).

By analysis of tree rings and fire scars, Mensing (1992) concluded that the structure of a blue oak woodland in Kern County resulted from changes in land use practices accompanying European settlement, with a period of high regeneration and recruitment associated with fire and browsing in the mid-1800s. McClaran and

Bartolome (1989) also concluded that an increase in fire frequency around the time of European settlement had caused an increase in recruitment. More recent studies have noted that fire can kill the tops of saplings, which then resprout. The resulting even-aged cohorts do not necessarily denote that fire has a positive impact on growth or recruitment (Bartolome and others 2002, Swiecki and Bernhardt 2002). Larger blue oak trees are fairly resistant to fire (Horney and others 2002).

The stand structure of blue oak woodlands is very distinctive, often composed of widely spaced trees over a grassy understory (fig. 5). The blue oak woodlands of California had the lowest basal area density of any of the common hardwood forest types: 68 percent of this forest type had less than 50 square feet per acre of basal area, and less than 4 percent had more than 100 square feet per acre of basal area (fig. 6). Blue oak woodlands were fairly pure in tree species composition, with 78 percent of the basal area in blue oak trees. Other tree species found in this type included ghost pine with 11 percent of total tree basal area and interior live oak with 5 percent of tree basal area. Vegetation found in this forest type included grasses, poison oak (*Toxicodendron diversilobum*), buckbrush (*Ceanothus cuneatus*), mountain mahogany (*Cercocarpus betuloides*), red-stem filaree (*Erodium cicutarium*), greenleaf manzanita (*Arctostaphylos patula*), whiteleaf manzanita (*Arctostaphylos viscida*), toyon (*Heteromeles arbutifolia*), California juniper (*Juniperus californica*), hollyleaf redberry (*Rhamnus crocea*), silver hairgrass (*Aira caryophyllea*), California scrub oak (*Quercus dumosa*), oat (*Avena* spp.), miner's lettuce (*Claytonia perfoliata*), fragrant bedstraw (*Galium triflorum*), common manzanita (*Arctostaphylos manzanita*), and others.

Most blue oak trees were relatively small, although individual blue oaks are capable of reaching large size. The average diameter at breast height (d.b.h.) for blue oak trees pole size or larger was 8.3 inches. The largest blue oak tree in these inventories had a 49-inch d.b.h. The record blue oak tree for California—also the national champion for the species—has a d.b.h. of 88 in and a height of 112 feet (UFEI 2004). There were an estimated 43 million sawtimber-sized blue oak trees in the state (table 17). Blue oak trees were found in 972,000 acres of other forest types, as shown in the tabulation on page 9[2].

---

[2] Estimate of amount of a forest type with a particular tree species present is affected by plot size, subplot configuration, whether fixed- or variable-radius sampling is used, and the practice of mapping condition boundaries. Any tree of the species, including seedlings, was used to determine species presence. Values for this forest type will differ from table 2 because not all trees within a plot are sampled.

Figure 5—A common stand structure for blue oak woodlands is scattered trees over a grassy understory. Regeneration is typically sparse.

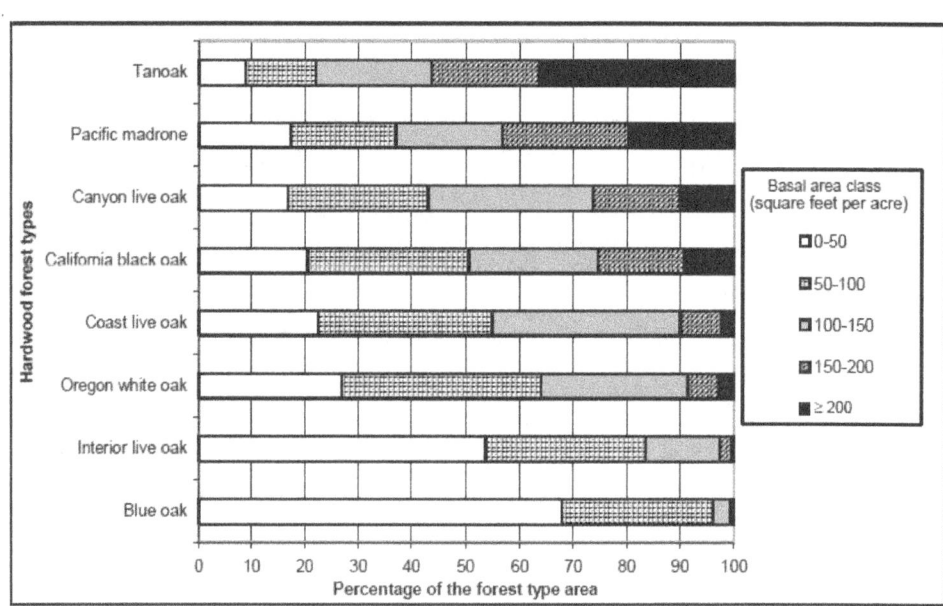

Figure 6—Relative basal area density of common hardwood forest types. Basal area was calculated from trees greater than 5 inches diameter at breast height.

Forest type with blue oak trees	Area	Sampling error	Percentage of all types with blue oak trees
	--- Thousand acres ---		
Blue oak/ghost pine	2,804	156	74
Interior live oak	554	94	15
Coast live oak	92	34	2
California buckeye	74	36	2
Canyon live oak	70	38	2
California black oak	59	25	2
Valley oak	33	22	1
Other	90	25	2
Total	3,776	162	100

Bolsinger (1988) found that blue oak was one of the tree species that appeared to have poor natural regeneration; other researchers have made similar observations (for example, Muick and Bartolome 1987). The 1990s forest inventories also provided evidence of sparse regeneration for blue oak. One metric that can be used to examine regeneration is the ratio of numbers of small saplings (1 to 3 inches d.b.h.) to numbers of medium saplings (3 to 5 inches d.b.h.). The sustainability of blue oak depends on many factors that are not captured in this metric, including growth and mortality rates, the periodicity of regeneration, and land conversion. However, a diameter-class ratio that is less than 1.0 is one indication of poor regeneration. For blue oak, the estimated ratio of 1- to 3-inch diameter trees to 3- to 5-inch diameter trees for the blue oak population in California was 0.7 (±26 percent se). Although other diameter-class ratios for small blue oak trees were greater than 1, the species had a relatively flat diameter distribution (table 18).

One of the metrics used to evaluate regeneration in the 1980s was regeneration stocking. The stocking classification used then could not be duplicated for this assessment because of changes in the sampling design. We applied a similar classification to plots with at least 90 percent of the plot area in the blue oak forest type. The following tabulation shows the proportion of this area stocked with trees less than 5 inches d.b.h. (blue oak seedlings and saplings). (See "regeneration stocking" in glossary for definitions of stocking class.)

The 1990s inventories found sparse regeneration of blue oak.

Stocking class	Area	Sampling error	Percentage of total
	– – Thousand acres – –		
Blue oak forest type evaluated for regeneration stocking:			
Nonstocked	502	88	29
Lightly stocked	825	111	48
Moderately stocked	331	71	19
Well stocked	54	37	3
All	1,712	148	100

Blue oak saplings (trees between 1 and 5 inches d.b.h.) can be old enough that many people would not consider them regeneration. The following tabulation shows the regeneration stocking classification applied to the same plots but using only seedlings (trees less than 1 inch d.b.h.).

Seedling stocking class	Area	Sampling error	Percentage of total
	– – Thousand acres – –		
Blue oak forest type evaluated for regeneration stocking:			
Nonstocked	746	104	43
Lightly stocked	706	104	41
Moderately stocked	224	59	13
Well stocked	36	32	2
All	1,712	148	100

If three subplots (rather than five) are used in evaluating stocking, as was done for the 1980s inventory, the estimated nonstocked area for seedlings is about 60 percent for both the 1980s inventory and the 1990s inventories.

All of the metrics used to evaluate regeneration—diameter-class ratios, stocking classification, and trees-per-acre estimates—showed that the sparse regeneration of blue oak continued into the 1990s. The long-term sustainability of blue oak woodlands is affected by many factors, and causal relationships are often best understood through designed research studies. However, regeneration of blue oak continues to be a concern and an important subject for future monitoring.

Canyon Live Oak Forest Type

Canyon live oak forest was the second most common inventoried hardwood forest type in California, estimated at 1.63 million acres (±6.3 percent se). The forest type was widely distributed, being found in the Klamath, Cascade, North Coast, Sierra Nevada, Transverse, and Peninsular Ranges (fig. 7). Canyon live oak trees were

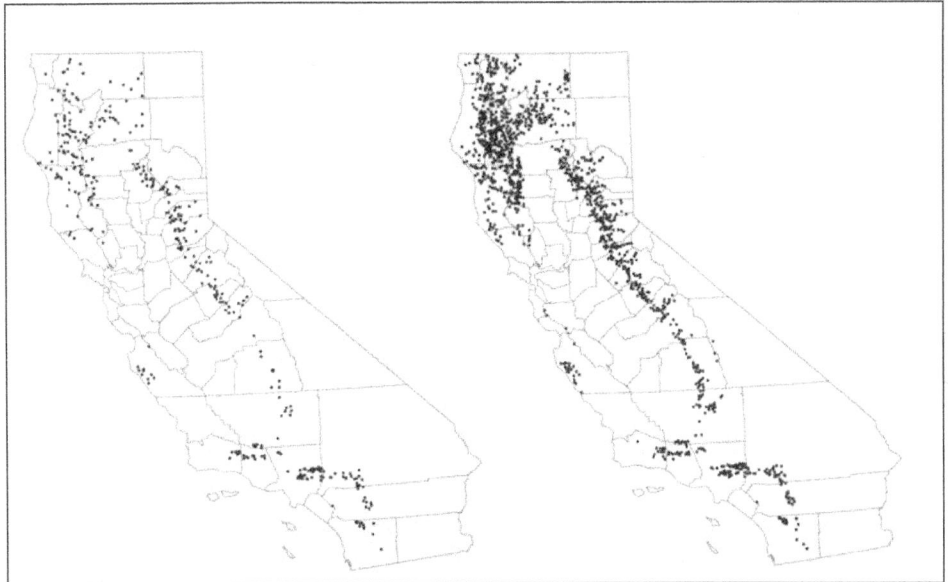

Figure 7—Sample plot locations for the canyon live oak (*Quercus chrysolepis*) forest type (left) and for canyon live oak trees (right). Figure includes plots for all inventories used in this report, and the plots shown did not all have the same probability of selection. To protect landowner privacy, each plot shown has some deliberate location error.

found extensively in other forest types (fig. 7). The canyon live oak forest type was estimated to have a mean elevation of 3,180 feet, with two-thirds of this forest type within an elevation range of 1,780 to 4,600 feet. The median average annual precipitation for this forest type was 42 inches per year, with two-thirds of the forest type found in areas with 35 to 53 inches of precipitation per year. It was one of the few hardwood forest types found primarily on national forests (61 percent), with 32 percent of the forest in private ownership and 7 percent in other public ownership.

Canyon live oak forest was distributed fairly evenly across low and moderate density classes (fig. 6). The most common tree species in the canyon live oak forest type were canyon live oak (59 percent of total tree basal area), Douglas-fir (*Pseudotsuga menziesii*) (13 percent), California black oak (6 percent), ponderosa pine (*Pinus ponderosa*) (4 percent), Pacific madrone (4 percent), incense cedar (*Calocedrus decurrens*) (3 percent), sugar pine (*Pinus lambertiana*) (2 percent), tanoak (2 percent), and California laurel (2 percent). Nontree vegetation occurring in the canyon live oak forest type included poison oak, toyon, whiteleaf manzanita, western swordfern (*Polystichum munitum*), western brackenfern (*Pteridium aquilinum*), California honeysuckle (*Lonicera hispidula*), California nutmeg (*Torreya californica*), and other forbs and shrubs.

Canyon live oak was the most numerous hardwood tree species.

Canyon live oak was the most numerous hardwood tree species in California forest lands, with an estimated 2.22 billion trees (±4 percent se). For these inventories, the canyon live oak tree with the largest diameter had a d.b.h. of 68 inches. The average tree size for this species was 8.5 inches, excluding seedlings and saplings. The record big tree for this species is 110 inches d.b.h. and 69 feet tall (UFEI 2004). However, only 2.3 percent of all canyon live oak trees were of sawtimber size (d.b.h. ≥11 inches). Canyon live oak trees were found in many forest types, including a number of timberland types. Of the 6 million acres of forest land where canyon live oak trees were found (see footnote 2), 76 percent was classified as timberland rather than woodland, and 36 percent was in private ownership.

Forest type with canyon live oak trees	Area	Sampling error	Percentage of all types with canyon live oak trees
	– – – Thousand acres – – –		
Mixed conifer	2,129	99	35
Canyon live oak	1,621	103	27
California black oak	515	55	9
Tanoak	323	45	5
Douglas-fir	296	40	5
Pacific madrone	191	38	3
Interior live oak	185	56	3
Ponderosa pine	163	30	3
Oregon white oak	97	30	2
Blue oak	80	30	1
Coast live oak	57	17	1
California laurel	48	22	1
Other	336	48	6
All types	6,039	173	100

The statewide population of canyon live oak appeared to be regenerating well. The estimated ratio of 1- to 3-inch diameter trees to 3- to 5-inch diameter trees for the canyon live oak population in California was 1.97 (±40 percent se). Other diameter-class ratios for small canyon live oak trees were also high (table 18). Within the canyon live oak forest type, the majority of plots were classified as well stocked or moderately stocked with either canyon live oak seedlings or canyon live oak saplings.

Stocking class	Area	Sampling error	Percentage of total
	– – – Thousand acres – – –		
Canyon live oak area evaluated for regeneration stocking:			
Nonstocked	70	21	6
Lightly stocked	196	45	18
Moderately stocked	429	59	39
Well stocked	395	53	36
All	1,090	91	100

California Black Oak Forest Type

California black oak is one of the most important hardwood tree species in the state. It is valued for aesthetics, for shade, for firewood, for lumber, and for the numerous acorns ("mast") that can be produced by mature trees. There was an estimated 1.25 million acres (±7 percent se) of the California black oak forest type in the state, excluding reserved lands outside of national forests. This forest type was evenly split between public ownership (50 percent) and private ownership. Seventy-seven percent of this type was classified as timberland. It was the third most common forest type, yet black oak trees had the greatest volume of any hardwood species in the state, with a total estimated volume of 5.1 billion cubic feet (table 6). Although occasionally used for lumber, California black oaks are primarily harvested for firewood. California black oak is important for wildlife because acorns provide a food source for many species. In one case study, researchers found mature black oak trees produced more than 6,000 acorns per oak, or 125,000 acorns per acre (Bowyer and Bleich 1980).

Plot data showed that this forest type and individual black oak trees have a wide distribution (fig. 8). The average elevation for the black oak forest type was 3,280 feet, with two-thirds of the forest occurring between 1,890 feet and 5,050 feet. The median average annual precipitation for this forest type was 45 inches per year, with two-thirds of the forest type found in areas with 39 to 52 inches of precipitation per year.

The California black oak forest type was well distributed across a range of low and moderate densities (fig. 6). The most common tree in this forest type was California black oak (47 percent of total tree basal area), followed by Douglas-fir (14 percent), incense cedar (8 percent), ponderosa pine (8 percent), canyon live oak (6 percent), Pacific madrone (4 percent), white fir (*Abies concolor*) (3 percent), and Oregon white oak (2 percent). Nontree plants in this forest type included

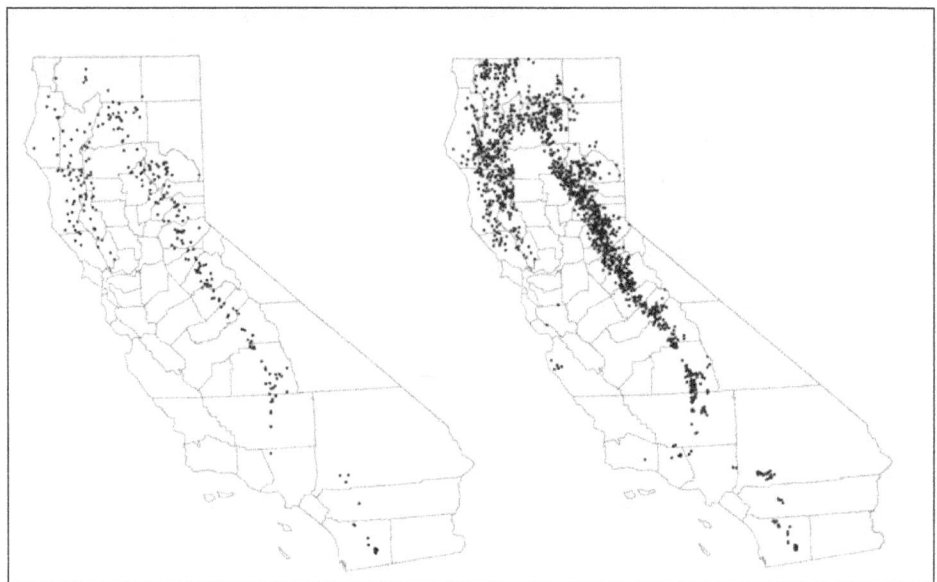

Figure 8—Sample plot locations for the California black oak (*Quercus kelloggii*) forest type (left) and for California black oak trees (right). Figure includes plots for all inventories used in this report, and the plots shown did not all have the same probability of selection. To protect landowner privacy, each plot shown has some deliberate location error.

poison oak, grass, deerbrush (*Ceanothus integerrimus*), sticky whiteleaf manzanita, western brackenfern, greenleaf manzanita, snowberry (*Symphoricarpos* spp.), California redbud (*Cercis occidentalis*), wood rose (*Rosa gymnocarpa)*, bear clover (*Chamaebatia foliolosa*), and other shrubs and forbs.

Although an estimated 1.25 million acres was classified as California black oak forest type, California black oak trees were typically a component of other forest types and were found on an estimated 7.21 million acres (±2 percent se) of forest land (see footnote 2). Of the total forest land where California black oak trees were found, 3.52 million acres (±4 percent se) was on private land, 3.49 million acres (±3 percent se) was on national forest, and 0.21 million acres (±17 percent se) was on other public land. Of the forest land where California black oak trees were found, 82 percent was classified as timberland. As shown in the tabulation below, California black oak trees were found in many different forest types.

Forest type with California black oak trees	Area	Sampling error	Percentage of all types with California black oak trees
	-- Thousand acres --		
Mixed conifer	3,317	119	46
California black oak	1,255	89	17
Canyon live oak	659	64	9
Ponderosa pine	380	43	5
Oregon white oak	293	55	4
Interior live oak	210	51	3
Douglas-fir	202	35	3
Pacific madrone	172	36	2
Blue oak	165	47	2
Tanoak	96	24	1
Other	462	59	6
All	7,211	179	100

California black oak was estimated to occur on less than 75,000 acres of each of the forest types included in "other," which consists of coast live oak, California laurel, valley oak, white fir, California buckeye, white alder, bigleaf maple, giant sequoia, bigcone Douglas-fir, Jeffrey pine, knobcone pine, red alder, coulter pine, and black cottonwood forest types.

There were an estimated 1.1 billion (±4.4 percent se) California black oak trees in forests within the state, excluding reserved lands outside of national forests. The largest California black oak tree in these inventories had a d.b.h. of 65 inches. The record big tree for the species has a 76-inch diameter and is 85 feet tall (UFEI 2004). Of the estimated 59.6 million (±5 percent se) sawtimber sized (≥11 inches d.b.h.) California black oak trees, 11 percent had d.b.h. ≥23 inches, and 4 percent had d.b.h. ≥29 inches (table 17). Seedling and sapling stocking of black oak appeared to be moderate within the California black oak forest type, as shown in the tabulation below.

Stocking class	Area	Sampling error	Percentage of total
	---- Thousand acres ----		
California black oak area evaluated for regeneration stocking:			
Nonstocked	217	43	26
Lightly stocked	243	37	29
Moderately stocked	246	40	29
Well stocked	131	34	16
All	837	75	100

Although this tabulation only shows regeneration within the California black oak type, California black oak is very frequently part of mixed-species stands. McDonald and Tappeiner (2002) report regeneration is generally highest under mature black oaks. Another regeneration metric, which is independent of forest type, is the overall diameter distribution across all forest types. For a given species, when there are fewer small trees than large trees statewide, it is an indirect indication that recruitment may not be sufficient to replace mortality. California black oak had a relatively flat diameter distribution for small trees between 1 and 11 inches d.b.h. (table 18), although all ratios of 2-inch diameter classes were above 1.0. Where natural regeneration is problematic, planting of black oaks can be a successful alternative (McDonald and Tappeiner 2002).

Tanoak is found in areas with high precipitation.

Tanoak Forest Type

The fourth most common hardwood forest type in California was tanoak, estimated to occur on 1.25 million acres (±6 percent se), excluding reserved lands outside of national forests. Tanoak is not in the oak genus (*Quercus*), but it is in the oak family (Fagaceae) and produces acorns. Most of the tanoak forest type in this inventory was found in the coastal counties north of San Francisco, with lesser amounts in the northern Sierra Nevada and central coastal counties (fig. 9). Average elevation for this forest type was 1,690 feet, with two-thirds of the forest type occurring between 750 and 2,600 feet elevation. Of all the common hardwood forest types, tanoak was found in areas of the greatest annual average precipitation (figs. 9 and 10). The median average annual precipitation for this forest type was 65 inches per year, with two-thirds of the forest type found in areas with 52 to 71 inches of precipitation per year. Eighty-two percent of this forest type was in private ownership, and 18 percent was in national forest ownership.

The distribution of tanoaks has waned and waxed and waned again since European settlement. After the California gold rush, tanoaks were used extensively to supply bark for tannin, leading to fears it was being overharvested. Tanoak provides an attractive wood that is used for flooring, paneling, veneer, and other products, but despite occasional attempts to develop markets for the wood, it has never been extensively used for this purpose. In the second half of the 20th century, selective harvesting of the more valuable conifers, accompanied by rapid sprouting and regrowth of tanoak, led to fears of conversion of previously conifer-dominated areas to tanoak. Although too recent to be reflected in the inventories used for this report, the fortunes of tanoak have once again taken a downward turn, because the

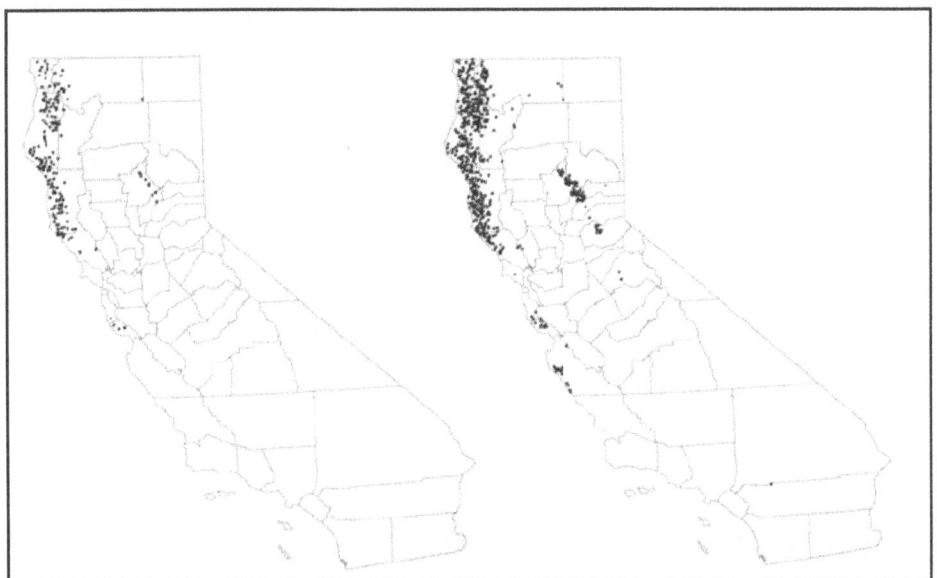

Figure 9—Sample plot locations for the tanoak (*Lithocarpus densiflora*) forest type (left) and for tanoak trees (right). Figure includes plots for all inventories used in this report, and the plots shown did not all have the same probability of selection. To protect landowner privacy, each plot shown has some deliberate location error.

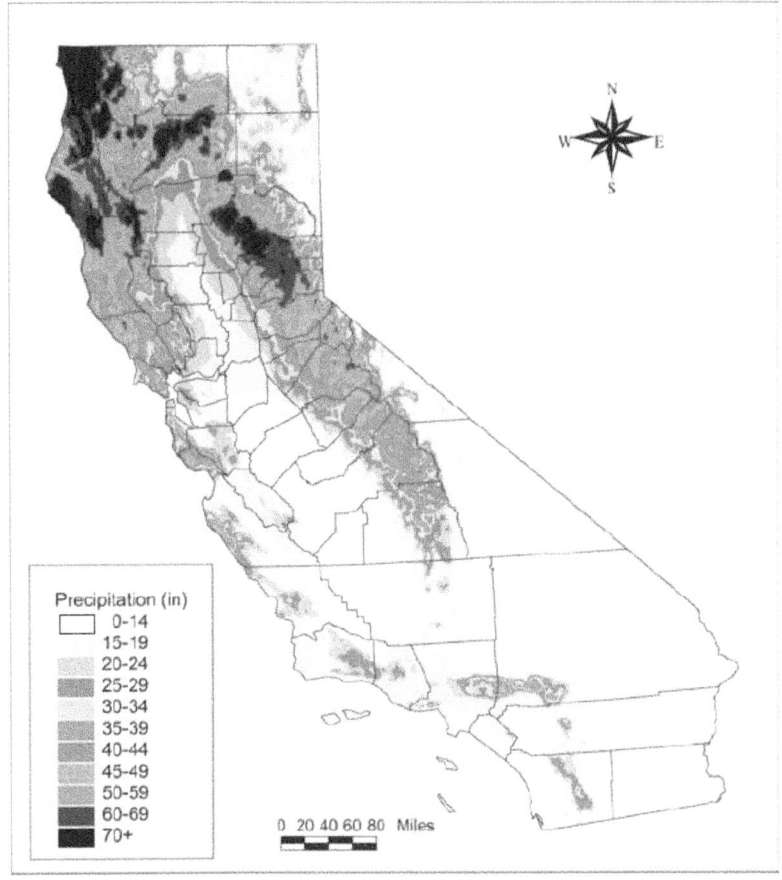

Figure 10—Annual precipitation for California, averaged for 1961 to 1990. Map produced with data from the Spatial Climate Analysis Service (2004).

effects of sudden oak death seem to be particularly severe for this species (Rizzo and Garbelotto 2003). Tanoak is an important resource for many wildlife species, providing both cover and food.

Tanoak forest was the densest of the common hardwood forest types (fig. 6). Within tanoak forest, the predominant tree species were tanoak (51 percent of total tree basal area), Douglas-fir (19 percent), redwood (*Sequoia sempervirens*) (11 percent), Pacific madrone (9 percent), canyon live oak (2 percent), and others (all at 1 percent or less of tree basal area). Nontree vegetation that was found on plots in the tanoak forest type included California huckleberry (*Vaccinium ovatum*), grass, western brackenfern, western swordfern, salal (*Gaultheria shallon*), poison oak, whipplea (*Whipplea modesta*), blueblossom ceanothus (*Ceanothus thyrsiflorus*), coast rhododendron (*Rhododendron macrophyllum*), redwood sorrel (*Oxalis oregana*), iris (*Iris* spp.), hairy manzanita (*Arctostaphylos columbiana*), starflower (*Trientalis latifolia*), Pacific wax-myrtle (*Myrica californica*), deerbrush, coast whitethorn (*Ceanothus incanus*), baccharis (*Baccharis* spp.), California honeysuckle, wood rose, whitebark raspberry (*Rubus leucodermis*), California red huckleberry (*Vaccinium parvifolium*), California hazelnut (*Corylus cornuta*), mountain-grape (*Berberis aquifolium*), California nutmeg, toyon, thimbleberry (*Rubus parviflorus*), and other shrubs and forbs.

Of the estimated 3.59 million acres (±3 percent se) where tanoak trees were found, 69 percent was in private ownership (see footnote 2). Ninety-nine percent of the area where tanoak trees were found was classified as timberland, where estimated potential productivity was at least 20 cubic feet per acre per year. The estimated area where tanoak trees were part of the forest was substantially larger than the estimate for the tanoak forest type. Where tanoak was not itself the predominant species, tanoak trees were typically found in conifer forest rather than hardwood forest, as shown in the tabulation below.

Forest type with tanoak trees	Area	Sampling error	Percentage of all types with tanoak trees
	– – – *Thousand acres* – – –		
Tanoak	1,249	80	35
Redwood	599	59	17
Douglas-fir	534	55	15
Mixed conifer	487	50	14
Canyon live oak	175	36	5
Pacific madrone	175	34	5
California black oak	82	22	2
California laurel	70	23	2
Other	214	36	6
All	3,585	99	100

"Other" forest types where tanoak was found included Oregon white oak, red alder, bigleaf maple, coast live oak, ponderosa pine, knobcone pine, interior live oak, giant chinquapin, and Bishop pine.

The record big tree for tanoak in California has an 86-inch d.b.h. and is 92 feet tall (UFEI 2004); the largest tree sampled in our inventory had a 62-inch d.b.h. and was 89 feet tall. Despite this potential for very large trees, of the estimated 53 million (±7 percent) sawtimber sized tanoak trees with d.b.h. ≥11 inches, only 6 percent of trees had d.b.h. ≥23 inches and only 1 percent had d.b.h. ≥29 inches.

All of the diameter-class ratios for small tanoak trees were above 1.5, which is one indication of good regeneration for the population as a whole (table 18). Using a stocking algorithm for tanoak seedlings or saplings in tanoak forest provided similar results: none of the area evaluated was nonstocked, 6 percent was lightly stocked, 44 percent was moderately stocked, and 50 percent was well stocked.

Interior Live Oak Forest Type

Interior live oak was a common hardwood forest type, with an estimated 1.14 million acres (±9 percent se) in California excluding reserved lands outside of national forests. Plot locations where the forest type was found and where interior live oak trees were found (fig. 11) were similar to the distribution of blue oak but were at slightly higher elevations and extended further south, and there were fewer samples found in the coastal counties. Average elevation for the forest type was 2,140 feet, with two-thirds of the forest type found between 1,200 and 3,100 feet. The median average annual precipitation for this forest type was 29 inches per year, with two-thirds of the forest type found in areas with 25 to 33 inches of precipitation per year. The interior live oak forest type was estimated to be 78 percent privately owned, 14 percent in national forest ownership, and 9 percent in other public ownership.

Like blue oak forest, interior live oak forest was very open, with 54 percent of area in the 0 to 50 square feet per acre basal area class (fig. 6). This forest type was primarily composed of hardwoods but had some conifers present: 68 percent of total tree basal area was in interior live oak trees, 8 percent was in blue oak trees, 7 percent was in ghost pine, 3 percent was in ponderosa pine, 2 percent was in Douglas-fir, and 2 percent was in canyon live oak. Nontree vegetation in this forest type that was found during the inventory included grass, poison oak, toyon, sticky whiteleaf manzanita, buckbrush, fragrant bedstraw, hollyleaf redberry, and other

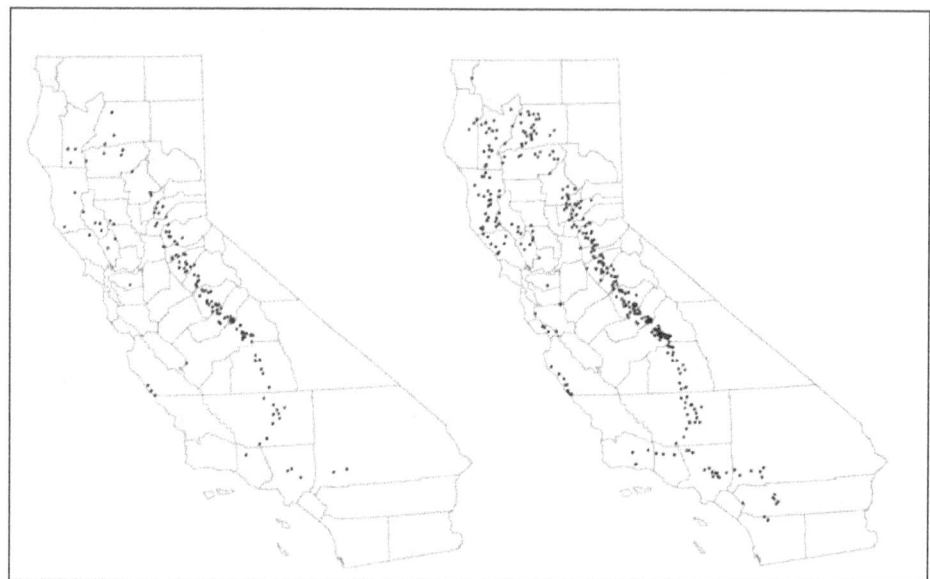

Figure 11—Sample plot locations for the interior live oak (*Quercus wislizeni*) forest type (left) and for interior live oak trees (right). Figure includes plots for all inventories used in this report, and the plots shown did not all have the same probability of selection. To protect landowner privacy, each plot shown has some deliberate location error.

forbs and shrubs. Only 24 percent of the forest where interior live oak trees were found was classified as timberland. Trees were commonly found in a variety of forest types, as shown in the tabulation below (see footnote 2).

Forest type with interior live oak trees	Area	Sampling error	Percentage of all types with interior live oak trees
	--- Thousand acres ---		
Interior live oak	1,116	116	41
Blue oak	658	98	24
Mixed conifer	197	35	7
Canyon live oak	174	49	6
California black oak	156	37	6
Coast live oak	64	30	2
California buckeye	62	29	2
Pacific madrone	55	28	2
Ponderosa pine	51	18	2
California laurel	53	22	2
Other	157	31	6
Total	2,743	151	100

Of the total 2.7 million acres where interior live oak trees were found, 73 percent of the area was in private ownership, 20 percent was in national forest ownership, and 7 percent was in other public ownership. The national champion big tree for the interior live oak species has an 80-inch d.b.h., is 51 feet tall, and has a crown diameter of 73 feet (UFEI 2004). The largest diameter tree in this inventory had a 50-inch d.b.h. Of the estimated 12.8 million (±13 percent se) live oak trees with d.b.h. ≥11 in, 4 percent had d.b.h. ≥23 in and 2 percent had d.b.h. ≥29 in (table 17). As one indication of good regeneration for the population, the smaller diameter to larger diameter ratios by 2-inch diameter class ranged from 1.6 to 2.2 for seedlings and saplings (table 18). As compared to other California oak species, a stocking classification also provided evidence of fair regeneration of seedlings and saplings:

Stocking class	Area	Sampling error	Percentage of total
	_ _ _ _ _ Thousand acres _ _ _ _		
Interior live oak forest type evaluated for regeneration stocking:			
Nonstocked	17	10	2
Lightly stocked	298	60	41
Moderately stocked	316	69	43
Well stocked	103	40	14
All	733	104	100

Coast Live Oak Forest Type

The coast live oak forest type area was estimated as 1.07 million acres (±9 percent se) excluding reserved lands outside of national forests. The coast live oak forest type and coast live oak trees were distributed along the central and southern coastal counties (fig. 12). Of the common hardwood types, the coast live oak type was found at the lowest mean elevation (1,360 feet), with two-thirds of this forest type within an elevation range of 600 to 2,090 feet. After the blue oak forest type, this forest type had the lowest estimated average annual precipitation of the common forest types. The median average annual precipitation for this forest type was 23 inches per year, with two-thirds of the forest type found in areas with 21 to 25 inches of precipitation per year. The coast live oak forest type was 79 percent privately owned with 13 percent in national forests and 8 percent in other public ownership.

The coast live oak forest type was primarily a single species type: 78 percent of the total tree basal area was in coast live oak trees, 4 percent was in California laurel, 2 percent was in Pacific madrone, 2 percent was in Douglas-fir, 2 percent

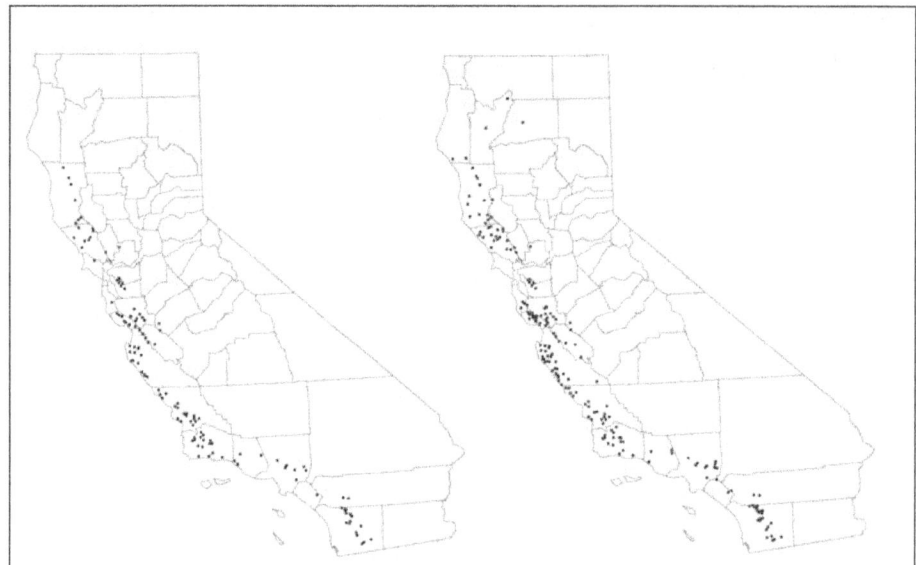

Figure 12—Sample plot locations for the coast live oak (*Quercus agrifolia*) forest type (left) and for coast live oak trees (right). Figure includes plots for all inventories used in this report, and the plots shown did not all have the same probability of selection. To protect landowner privacy, each plot shown has some deliberate location error.

was in valley oak, and 2 percent was in redwood trees. The coast live oak forest type was denser than the blue oak or interior live oak forest types, and less dense than the canyon live oak or California black oak forest types (fig. 6). Coast live oak trees were predominantly found in coast live oak forest, as shown in the tabulation below (see footnote 2).

Forest type with coast live oak trees	Area	Sampling error	Percentage of all types with coast live oak trees
	--- Thousand acres ---		
Coast live oak	1,059	88	66
Blue oak	89	28	6
Redwood	76	23	5
California laurel	68	27	4
Engelmann oak	54	16	3
Tanoak	48	20	3
Pacific madrone	39	20	2
California black oak	38	24	2
Bigleaf maple	23	13	1
Other	114	30	7
Total	1,609	102	100

The national champion tree for the coast live oak species is found in California and has a 108-inch d.b.h., height of 58 feet, and a crown diameter of 75 feet (UFEI 2004). The largest diameter tree in this inventory had a 69-inch d.b.h. and a height of 63 feet. Of the estimated 42 million coast live oak trees with d.b.h. ≥11 inches, 7 percent had a d.b.h. of at least 23 inches and 2 percent had a d.b.h. of at least 29 inches. The numbers of saplings by diameter class appeared variable (table 18) with a relatively flat distribution for trees with d.b.h. between 3 and 11 inches.

Oregon White Oak Forest Type

The Oregon white oak forest type area was estimated as 580,000 acres (±12 percent se) excluding reserved lands outside of national forests. Both the forest type and Oregon white oak trees were found primarily in the north Coast, Klamath, and Cascade Ranges (fig. 13). Oregon white oak forest type was found at an average elevation of 2,560 feet, with two-thirds of the forest found between 1,470 and 3,860 feet. The median average annual precipitation for this forest type was 49 inches per year, with two-thirds of the forest type found in areas with 39 to 58 inches of precipitation per year. It was a moderately open oak forest type–denser than blue oak or interior live oak forest, but less dense than canyon live oak forest (fig. 6). Ownership of the forest type was 74 percent private, 20 percent national forest, and 6 percent other public.

Within the Oregon white oak forest type, individual Oregon white oak trees contributed 63 percent of the total tree basal area. Other tree species found in this type included Douglas-fir (12 percent of total basal area), California black oak (9 percent), Pacific madrone (4 percent), ponderosa pine (4 percent), and canyon live oak (2 percent).

Total area where Oregon white oak trees were found was estimated at 1.47 million acres (±7 percent se) (see footnote 2). Fifty-eight percent of this area was privately owned, 36 percent was in national forest, and 6 percent was in other public ownership: 61 percent of this area was in the more productive timberland class. Oregon white oak trees were often found in the mixed-conifer type, as shown in the following tabulation.

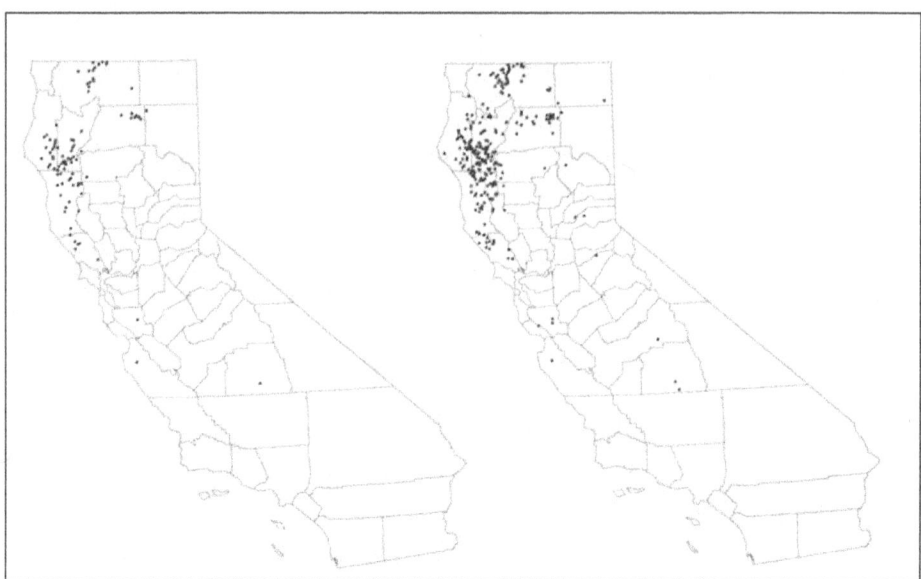

Figure 13—Sample plot locations for the Oregon white oak (*Quercus garryana*) forest type (left) and for Oregon white oak trees (right). Figure includes plots for all inventories used in this report, and the plots shown did not all have the same probability of selection. To protect landowner privacy, each plot shown has some deliberate location error.

Forest type with Oregon white oak trees	Area	Sampling error	Percentage of all types with Oregon white oak trees
	– – *Thousand acres* – –		
Oregon white oak	563	70	38
Mixed conifer	276	42	19
California black oak	155	32	10
Douglas-fir	85	24	6
Canyon live oak	65	22	5
Pacific madrone	60	22	4
Ponderosa pine	52	18	4
California laurel	48	24	3
Blue oak	35	14	2
Coast live oak	24	17	2
Other	102	28	7
Total	1,473	101	100

Regeneration for Oregon white oak appeared to be sparse.

Regeneration for Oregon white oak appeared to be sparse, although the relatively small number of sample plots introduced substantial sampling error. The estimated ratio of 1- to 3-inch diameter trees to 3- to 5-inch diameter trees for the Oregon white oak population in California was 0.7 ($\pm$73 percent se). Low to moderate regeneration was indicated by stocking of seedlings and saplings on 41 plots that had at least 90 percent of the area covered by Oregon white oak forest type.

Stocking class	Area	Sampling error	Percentage of total
	– – – – *Thousand acres* – – – –		
Oregon white oak forest type evaluated for regeneration stocking:			
Nonstocked	69	30	23
Lightly stocked	89	32	30
Moderately stocked	75	28	25
Well stocked	67	27	22
All	300	57	100

Pacific Madrone Forest Type

The Pacific madrone forest type was estimated to be just 3 percent of all hardwood forests, or 348,000 acres (±15 percent se). However, madrone was fairly common as a component of other forests (fig. 14), making up 9 percent of all the hardwood sawtimber trees in the state (table 17). Next to tanoak, Pacific madrone forest was the densest of hardwood forest types (fig. 6). Madrone forest was found at an average elevation of 1,930 feet, with two-thirds of the forest type occurring between elevations of 910 feet and 3,020 feet. After the tanoak forest type, the madrone forest type had the second greatest average annual rainfall of common hardwoods. The median average annual precipitation for this forest type was 54 inches per year, with two-thirds of the for-est type found in areas with 39 to 58 inches of precipitation per year.

Pacific madrone is typically found in mixed-species forests.

Douglas-fir was the most common associated species within the Pacific madrone forest type, as indicated by the distribution of tree basal area: madrone (37 percent of total tree basal area), Douglas-fir (26 percent), tanoak (11 percent), canyon live oak (7 percent), California black oak (7 percent), California laurel (3 percent), and other species (each at 1 percent or less of total tree basal area). Private ownership of the madrone forest was estimated at 215,000 (±21 percent se), which was 62 percent of the forest type. National forests accounted for 35 percent of the forest type, and other public ownership was estimated as 3 percent of the madrone forest.

Madrone trees were estimated to have occurred on 3.9 million acres (±4 percent se) of inventoried forest land (see footnote 2), where 55 percent was privately owned, 41 percent was in national forest ownership, and 4 percent was in other public ownership. Madrone was most commonly found in the tanoak forest type, as shown in the tabulation below.

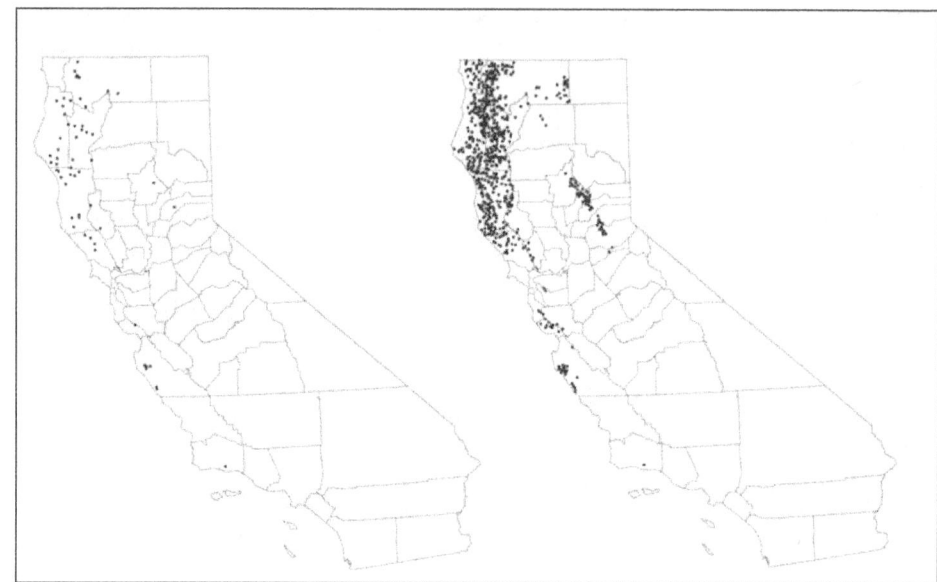

Figure 14—Sample plot locations for Pacific madrone (*Arbutus menziesii*) forest type (left) and for Pacific madrone trees (right). Figure includes plots for all inventories used in this report, and the plots shown did not all have the same probability of selection. To protect landowner privacy, each plot shown has some deliberate location error.

Forest type with Pacific madrone trees	Area	Sampling error	Percentage of all types with Pacific madrone trees
	– – – Thousand acres – – –		
Tanoak	967	73	25
Mixed conifer	804	62	21
Douglas-fir	428	49	11
Pacific madrone	348	54	9
Canyon live oak	299	47	8
Redwood	239	42	6
California black oak	237	42	6
Coast live oak	182	47	5
Oregon white oak	105	36	3
California laurel	89	28	2
Other types	215	40	5
Total	3,912	137	100

The national champion tree for Pacific madrone is found in California, and it has a 57-inch diameter, is 92 feet high, and has a crown diameter of 70 feet (UFEI 2004). In California, there were an estimated 32 million (±7 percent se) madrone sawtimber trees with d.b.h. ≥11 inches (table 17). Only 10 percent of sawtimber trees had d.b.h. ≥23 inches, and 3 percent of sawtimber trees had d.b.h. ≥29 inches.

The ratio of numbers of seedlings relative to 1- to 3-inch d.b.h. trees and the ratio of number of 1- to 3-inch d.b.h. trees to 3- to 5-inch d.b.h. trees were both above 2.0 (table 18), which is one indication of good regeneration for the madrone population in the state.

Other Hardwood Forest Types

All of the other hardwood forest types in California were relatively uncommon. The next most common type after madrone, California laurel, was less than 2 percent of the total hardwood forest area in California. This uncommon forest type was only found on 27 plots, which presented some difficulty in making a meaningful assessment of characteristics like density, species composition, or regeneration. However, the inventory does provide good evidence that these types were indeed uncommon.

Another uncommon oak forest type was the valley oak forest type, estimated at 152,000 acres (±29 percent se), or just 1.3 percent of total hardwood forest area. Engelmann oak (*Quercus engelmannii*) forest type is also rare estimated at 63,000 acres (±41 percent se), which is just one-half of one percent of all hardwood forest. For both of these types, only very sparse regeneration (seedlings and saplings) was found in the corresponding sample plots, but we do not have enough data to know whether this was true for the statewide population. Estimates for all forest types are shown in table 2. If sampling error is 100 percent or if forest types were not present in the sample, it is likely that there were fewer than 100,000 acres of forest in California where that tree species was predominant.

Hardwoods are highly important to diversity of wildlife.

Hardwood Resources

Wildlife

Hardwoods, and oak species in particular, are highly important to the diversity of wildlife found in California. About 110 bird species occupy California oak habitats during breeding season (Verner 1980). Barrett (1980) described the many ways mammals use oaks: hollow trees, logs, and roots serve as denning sites; small and large herbivores forage on leaves and twigs; oaks may support fungi, mistletoe, or insects used by mammals; and of greatest impact, oaks produce acorns, which serve as a food source for many animals.

The California wildlife habitat relationships system (CDFG 2002) indicates acorns are an essential habitat element for acorn woodpeckers (fig. 15). Fifty vertebrate wildlife species are listed as using acorns (CDFG 2002):

Mammals	Birds
Bighorn sheep (*Ovis canadensis*)	Acorn woodpecker (*Melanerpes formicivorus*)
Black bear (*Ursus americanus*)	
Brush mouse (*Peromyscus boylii*)	Band-tailed pigeon (*Columba fasciata*)
California chipmunk (*Tamias obscurus*)	California quail (*Callipepla californica*)
Cal. ground squirrel (*Spermophilus beecheyi*)	California thrasher (*Toxostoma redivivum*)
California mouse (*Peromyscus californicus*)	Gila woodpecker (*Melanerpes uropygialis*)
Deermouse (*Peromyscus maniculatus*)	Gilded flicker (*Colaptes chrysoides*)
Desert cottontail (*Sylvilagus audubonii*)	Hairy woodpecker (*Picoides villosus*)
Desert woodrat (*Neotoma lepida*)	Island scrub-jay (*Aphelocoma insularis*)
Douglas' squirrel (*Tamiasciurus douglasii*)	Juniper titmouse (*Baeolophus griseus*)
Dusky-footed woodrat (*Neotoma fuscipes*)	Lewis' woodpecker (*Melanerpes lewis*)
Eastern fox squirrel (*Sciurus niger*)	Mountain quail (*Oreortyx pictus*)
Eastern gray squirrel (*Sciurus carolinensis*)	Northern flicker (*Colaptes auratus*)
Elk (*Cervus elaphus*)	Oak titmouse (*Baeolophus inornatus*)
Island gray fox (*Urocyon littoralis*)	Sandhill crane (*Grus canadensis*)
Long-eared chipmunk (*Tamias quadrimaculatus*)	Spotted towhee (*Pipilo maculatus*)
Merriam's chipmunk (*Tamias merriami*)	Steller's jay (*Cyanocitta stelleri*)
Mule deer (*Odocoileus hemionus*)	Varied thrush (*Ixoreus naevius*)
Northern flying squirrel (*Glaucomys sabrinus*)	Western scrub-jay (*Aphelocoma californica*)
Pinyon mouse (*Peromyscus truei*)	White-breasted nuthatch (*Sitta carolinensis*)
Raccoon (*Procyon lotor*)	
Rock squirrel (*Spermophilus variegatus*)	Wild turkey (*Meleagris gallopavo*)
Siskiyou chipmunk (*Tamias siskiyou*)	Wood duck (*Aix sponsa*)
Sonoma chipmunk (*Tamias sonomae*)	Yellow-billed magpie (*Pica nuttalli*)
Virginia opossum (*Didelphis virginiana*)	
Western gray squirrel (*Sciurus griseus*)	
Wild pig (*Sus scrofa*)	
Yellow-cheeked chipmunk (*Tamias ochrogenys*)	

Most oaks produce abundant acorn crops intermittently, every 2 or 3 years or at irregular intervals, so that a diversity of oak species in an area can help regulate the food supply. Madrone trees provide wildlife food by producing extensive berry crops (fig. 16). Other parts of hardwood trees–shoots, buds, sap, and leaves–can serve as wildlife food, as can fungi and mistletoe species that live on hardwood trees. Over one-third of all bird species on hardwood rangelands make use of snags (Standiford 2001). Coarse woody debris, important for most reptiles and amphibians and many bird species (Standiford 2001), averaged 1.2 tons/acre for unreserved woodland outside of national forests (Tietje and others 2002).

Riparian habitat elements are used by almost 90 percent of all hardwood rangeland wildlife species (Standiford 2001). Hardwoods are also important to

Figure 15—The acorn woodpecker stores acorns in numerous small tree cavities, each large enough to hold a single acorn.

Figure 16—Berries on a Pacific madrone (*Arbutus menziesii*) tree.

invertebrates and aquatic vertebrates. The California Department of Forestry and Fire Protection estimates that 95 percent of the historical range of riparian forests has been lost (CDFFP 2003). Hardwood trees such as alder and maple are frequently more prevalent in riparian areas (fig. 17) and contribute to the coarse

Figure 17—Hardwoods such as this bigleaf maple (*Acer macrophyllum*) are often found along riparian areas.

woody debris in streams and lakes. Shade provided by hardwood trees is critical in moderating summer stream temperatures. Hardwood trees stabilize streambanks, help to prevent erosion, and contribute to preserving overall water quality.

Forest Product Resources

Alder, California black oak, bigleaf maple, tanoak, Pacific madrone, and Oregon white oak are all used to create manufactured forest products. These and other California hardwoods are used to make furniture, flooring, pallets, veneer, paneling, molding, fence posts, and other items. Parts of hardwood trees and other plants in hardwood forests are also used for many nontraditional forest products, ranging from food and medicinal products to dye and material for artwork or crafts.

The estimated net growing-stock volume of hardwood tree species on unreserved land was 14.1 billion cubic feet (±3 percent se) (table 3). Net growing-stock volume was calculated from a 12-inch-high stump to a 4-inch-diameter top for all trees greater than 5 inches d.b.h. and was adjusted to account for both sound and rotten culls. Sixty-five percent of unreserved growing-stock hardwood volume was on private lands, and 67 percent was on timberland rather than woodland.

Net growing-stock volume does not include all hardwood volume; some species were defined as live cull in some areas (for example, blue oak on national forests), and individual trees can be defined as cull because of their form. Utilization standards for some purposes (for example, bioenergy or pulp) may include small trees and tree tops that are not included in the net growing-stock estimate.

> **Oaks provide 90 percent of the tree biomass in woodland and 53 percent in timberland hardwood types.**

On unreserved forest land, the total sound hardwood volume, measured from the ground to the tree tip for trees greater than 4 inches d.b.h, was estimated as 23.48 billion cubic feet (±2 percent se). Sixty-nine percent of this volume was on private lands, and 61 percent was on timberland rather than woodland (table 10).

Estimates of biomass have been increasing in importance, in part because of the need to estimate carbon storage. Oaks provided 90 percent of the tree biomass in woodland (table 7) and 53 percent of tree biomass in timberland hardwood types (table 8). The aboveground biomass of hardwood trees on forest land was estimated as 555 million tons (±2 percent se) (table 9), or 29 percent of overall tree biomass.

For the year 2000, the estimated volume of hardwoods harvested for industrial use in California was 10.7 million board feet (MMBF) Scribner, distributed as 2.0 MMBF to sawmills, 2.7 MMBF burned for bioenergy (does not include firewood), and 6.0 MMBF for other products such as pulp and paper (Morgan and others 2004). This was about 0.5 percent of total California timber harvest volume (Morgan and others 2004). Since 1982, the hardwood proportion of annual harvest in California has typically ranged between 0.05 and 0.50 percent of all species harvested for industrial use in California (Morgan and others 2004). The volume of hardwoods harvested for industrial purposes in California would have been about 0.1 percent of the estimated 10,505 MMBF standing volume on unreserved lands. The relatively low rate of harvest for industrial purposes has led many authors to conclude that hardwoods are an underutilized resource (Delfino 1986, Huber and McDonald 1992). In recent years, an increase in west coast red alder prices, which now sometimes surpass Douglas-fir prices, has provided an example of the potential for relatively quick and dramatic changes in marketability of western hardwoods.

The volume harvested annually for industrial use in California was much smaller than the total annual volume harvested. Hardwood trees can be cut for many purposes: to clear land for building, range improvements, or agriculture; to harvest trees for firewood; or to reduce competition against more commercially valuable tree species. The total estimated annual harvest volume of hardwood trees at least 5 inches d.b.h. on unreserved lands outside national forests was 56.0 million cubic feet per year (table 14). The total estimated annual harvest volume of hardwood trees ≥11 inches d.b.h. on unreserved land outside national forests was 98 MMBF Scribner. When compared to the 2 MMBF annual harvest volume of hardwoods that goes to sawmills (Morgan and others 2004), it is apparent that only a small portion of harvested sawtimber-sized hardwood trees was milled as sawtimber.

The total periodic hardwood harvest volume of net growing stock on unreserved land outside of national forests from 1981-84 to 1991-94 was estimated as 2 percent of 1991-94 hardwood inventory volume on woodland and 7 percent of 1991-94 hardwood inventory volume on timberland. The total annual mortality volume of hardwoods that were harvested or culturally killed was 23 percent of annual gross growth (tables 14 and 15). It is unknown how much of the harvest volume was used for nonindustrial forest products such as firewood, and how much was treated as unusable material. More than 200,000 homes in California are primarily heated by wood (USDC Bureau of the Census 2004), and many more use wood as a secondary heating source. Hardwoods are valued as firewood because they burn slowly and form good coals.

Hardwood Rangeland

Clearing of oak woodlands and sparse regeneration are issues of concern.

The majority of California's woodlands are grazed. The 1981-84 inventory of unreserved woodland outside of national forests found that 55 percent of woodland plots were recorded as having evidence of grazing within the past year (Bolsinger 1988); because field visits occurred during different times of year and grazing would not always be apparent, this estimate was probably low. Corresponding with the 1981-84 woodland inventory, and selecting from private owners where oak species were predominant, a 1985 survey provided an estimate that 77 percent of private oak woodland was grazed (Huntsinger and Fortmann 1990); this rate might be high if owners did not graze all of their land. A range of 55 percent to 77 percent grazing for private woodland in the 1990s corresponds to 3 to 4 million acres. Publicly owned woodlands are also often commonly grazed, as are private and public savannas with less than 10 percent tree cover.

The 1985 statewide survey by Huntsinger and Fortmann was intended to aid education programs and included questions about landowner attitudes. The majority of owners who owned more than 5,000 acres valued oaks for shade, wildlife habitat, natural beauty, and fuelwood. A majority of owners of smaller land areas valued oaks for the same things plus property value and erosion control (Huntsinger and Fortmann 1990).

Between 1985 and 1992, a multiagency program (the Integrated Hardwood Range Management Program) engaged in an active program of research and education. A followup survey in 1992 of the same landowners surveyed in the 1985 survey found small but significant changes in responses: a decrease in the percentage of owners who have livestock grazing on their property; an increase in proximity to subdivisions; an increase in valuing oaks for erosion control, browse, and water conservation; decreases in the percentage of landowners who thinned oaks, cut oaks, or sold firewood; increases in planting or protecting oak sprouts; and an increase in owners who agreed that oaks were being lost in California (Huntsinger and others 1997).

How changes in attitudes or practices have affected oak woodlands is largely unknown. At the time of the 1981-84 inventory, a variety of evidence indicated problems with oak woodlands. Bolsinger (1988) aggregated State of California annual reports of timber harvest to estimate 1.9 million acres of hardwoods and chaparral had been cleared in rangeland improvement projects from 1945 to 1974. A number of oak species showed sparse regeneration, as they continue to do. Clearing of oak woodlands for development, for agriculture, for vineyards, and for subdivisions was noticeable in the 1980s and continued to be a focus of public concern in the 1990s. There are many case studies discussing problems with recruitment and retention of oaks.

Changes in California Hardwoods From 1981-84 to 1991-94

Methods

Because the spatial variability of forests is high, and mortality information requires tracking of individual trees, the best method for estimating change is to remeasure permanent plots over time. There were no remeasurement data for national forests or reserved lands for this time period. On other lands, woodland forest was not measured until the 1980s, and at that time the plot intensity was one plot per 30,000 acres. Most of the 1980s woodland plots were remeasured in the 1990s, but a change in inventory design resulted in a reduction of the number of remeasured trees.

This results in very uncertain estimates of how forests changed from the 1980s to the 1990s. For tables 13 to 16, estimates were made by using 773 timberland plots with hardwood trees and 189 remeasured woodland plots. Standard errors in tables and confidence intervals given in the text can be used to understand uncertainty related to sampling error.

For tables 11 and 12, change in forest type on woodland was estimated from all 345 plots installed in the 1990s, including those that had not had 1980s tree measurements. Where trees were measured for the first time in the 1990s, the 1980s measurements were modeled by using a process described in Waddell (1991). Air photos taken in the 1980s and 1990s exist for all plots and were useful in confirming changes between forest and nonforest.

The best method of estimating change is to remeasure permanent plots over time.

The estimates in this report apply 1990s methods (volume equations and forest type classification algorithms) to data from both periods to help ensure change estimates reflect real change rather than changes in the inventory and analysis procedures. All estimates in this report cannot be directly compared to those in the Bolsinger (1988) report because of changes in inventory design and estimation procedures. Readers interested in more detail about the estimation process for change should contact the authors.

Results

Overall, there was an estimated 3-percent decrease of unreserved woodland area outside national forests from the 1980s to the 1990s. The majority of this decrease (88 percent) was caused by a transfer of land to reserved or national forest status (table 11).

Only 2 of 345 oak woodland plots (0.6 percent) changed from woodland in 1981-84 to nonforest in 1991-94. One woodland plot was converted to urban (developed) land and one plot was converted to nonforest rangeland. Using this conversion information, we estimated that the 1980s to 1990s rate of conversion of woodland to nonforest on unreserved land outside of national forests was 29,000 acres per decade, with a 68 percent confidence interval (CI) of 11,000 to 69,000 acres per decade.[3] This estimate does not include conversion of oak savanna, where tree cover is less than 10 percent, to urban or agricultural conditions.

One of the 345 plots that was oak woodland in the 1980s burned in a wildfire and became chaparral, and one chaparral plot from the 1980s grew into an oak woodland classification. For each process (woodland changing to chaparral and chaparral changing to woodland), the estimated rates of change between 1981-84 and 1991-94 were 15,000 acres per decade, with a range of 4,000 to 51,000 acres per decade at a 68 percent CI. Because it can be difficult to draw a clear distinction between chaparral and oak woodland in all cases, it is possible that there may have been some classification error that is not included in this estimate.

If transfers out of the population are included, there was no net change in the area of hardwood forest on unreserved timberlands outside of national forests. If transfers are excluded, there was an estimated 2 percent increase in the area of hardwood timberland from 1981-84 to 1991-94.

---

[3] Estimates differ slightly from values in table 11 because stratification is not used.

Timberland change	Area	Additions	Subtractions	Net change
		Thousand acres		
1981-84 hardwood forest types	2,654			
Change to/from nonstocked forest		20	(15)	5
Change to/from softwood type		212	(144)	68
Conversion to/from nonforest		15	(30)	(15)
Transfer to national forests or reserved			(55)	(56)
Total change		247	(245)	2
1991-94 hardwood forest type	2,656			

Four plots changed from hardwood timberland to nonforest: three tanoak forest plots and one giant chinquapin plot were converted to developed land or roads. The estimated rate of conversion to nonforest from 1981-84 to 1991-94 for hardwood forest types on unreserved timberland was 30,000 acres per decade, with a range of 14,000 to 55,000 acres per decade using a 68 percent CI.

Table 12 shows estimates of change from 1981-84 to 1991-94 for individual forest types. Estimated area in a forest type can change for a variety of reasons. Conversion to nonforest was described above, and this is most likely the change that is of greatest concern to people. In other cases, land was transferred to national ownership or reserve status; these types of land were not part of the FIA inventory, and so plots that fell into this category were not remeasured. In yet other cases, plots changed from one forest type to another. A change in forest type might reflect substantial change on the plot—for example, selective harvesting of all conifers on the plot—or the change in forest type can occur with relatively small amounts of mortality or differential growth rates among trees of different species. Estimated areas for individual forest types that changed by large percentages were all relatively uncommon types, so that the 1991-94 estimate was within a sampling error of the 1981-84 type (table 12). For these types, the change shown reflects sampling error rather than real change. This does not mean that area for these types remained constant; it means that we simply do not know what change occurred.

One change estimate of interest is the decrease in the California black oak forest type. The California black oak forest type in 1981-84 was estimated at 751,000 acres (±11 percent se), and had a 12 percent net decrease for 1991-94, unadjusted for transfer to national forest or reserved status (table 12). Transfers or redefinitions of land to reserve status or national forest accounted for 37 percent of

Oaks and other hardwoods increased in net growing-stock volume.

the decrease. An estimated 15,000 acres shifted into the California black oak forest type (range 4,000 to 37,000 acres per decade at a 68 percent CI). An estimated 62,000 acres (8 plots) shifted out of the California black oak forest type to other forest types or to a nonstocked condition (range 40,000 to 88,000 acres per decade at a 68 percent CI). The eight plots showed the range of reasons for conversion of black oak to other forest types: two plots shifted to other types owing to higher growth in other species, one plot had black oaks die from natural causes, two plots had black oaks that were killed and left on site, one plot had black oaks harvested and removed, and fires burned over two plots, one of which was salvage logged. Excluding salvage logging, 11 percent of all black oak timberland plots had some black oak trees harvested or cut and left between 1981-84 and 1991-94; the corresponding estimate for the state would be 64,000 acres affected per decade.

Oaks and other hardwoods increased in net growing-stock volume between the 1980s and the 1990s (table 13). Estimated annual mortality volume for trees that were harvested or culturally killed was about the same as natural mortality (table 14) but overall mortality and removal volume was lower than gross annual growth (table 15). Significant net growth increases occurred for blue oak, California black oak, Oregon white oak, bigleaf maple, California laurel, Pacific madrone, and tanoak (table 15).

Pre-Sudden Oak Death Forest Conditions for 12 California Counties

By the end of 2003, 12 California counties had been quarantined for sudden oak death. These were Alameda, Contra Costa, Humboldt, Marin, Mendocino, Monterey, Napa, San Mateo, Santa Clara, Santa Cruz, Solano, and Sonoma Counties (fig. 18). As of spring 2004, the associated pathogen (*Phytophtora ramorum*) had also been found in isolated instances in additional counties in California and in Oregon and Washington. Within the range of areas where the disease is established, the distribution of the disease appears to be patchy (McPherson and others 2002). Initially symptom-free trees in affected areas can later develop the disease (McPherson and others 2002); in one case study, remote-sensing imagery suggested a continuing mortality rate of 0.4 trees per acre in an area where the disease was already established (Kelly and Meentemeyer 2002).

Active measures are in place to limit the spread of the disease, but the potential range is unknown. Although climate may play a role in limiting the disease, the pathogen has been found in a wide range of microclimates (Rizzo and others 2002). Portions of the Sierra Nevada, and additional areas of coastal forests in California and Oregon, are similar in species composition and environment to the currently

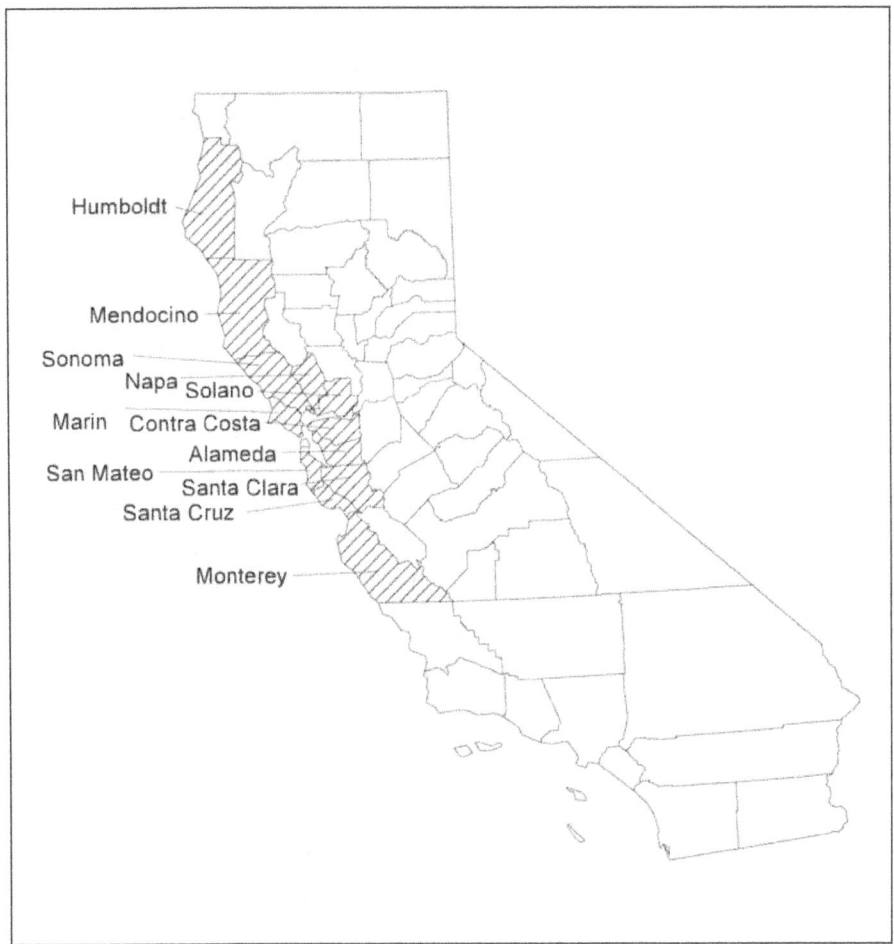

Figure 18—By spring of 2004, 12 counties in California were affected by the sudden oak death epidemic.

listed area. There are also large areas of the Central, Southern, and Eastern United States with tree species that might be susceptible to the disease. Because the eventual range of the disease is unknown, we have chosen to limit this assessment of pre-epidemic forest conditions to the 12-county area in California most affected in spring 2004.

The inventory plots used for this assessment will provide baseline information for future monitoring of the epidemic. The Forest Inventory and Analysis program is continuing to monitor forest change in the sudden oak death region in two ways: (1) within the ongoing inventory system, plots are being measured each year, and (2) FIA scientists are currently engaged in cooperative sudden oak death research projects that remeasure a subset of plots used in this assessment. The estimates given here are a pre-epidemic assessment of forest land in the 12-county area and do not include any estimate of disease occurrence or spread.

There were approximately 5.5 million acres of forest land in these 12 counties. This estimate is approximate, because some of the forest within these counties was unsampled prior to 2001, and the data collected after 2001 are not yet sufficient for analysis. This unsampled land consisted of reserved land outside of national forests, such as the southern portion of Redwoods National Park or the Point Reyes National Seashore. There were no field measurements for these areas, but from landowner or manager responses, the unsampled forest land would be 442,000 acres, or 8 percent of the total forest area in these counties (Waddell and Bassett 1996, 1997a, 1997b). In addition, this assessment is limited to the definition of forest land, which excludes lands with nonforest uses, such as city parks and residential areas.

Of the remaining 5.09 million acres of forest land in these counties, 87 percent was outside national forests and field measurements were taken during 1991-94. The remaining 13 percent of forest land had field measurements in 1996-98 and are from national forests in Humboldt, Mendocino, and Monterey Counties. As some tanoak deaths were reported as early as 1995, and the disease could have been present before the first reports, there is a possibility of temporal overlap between the incidence of the disease and the statistics reported here. However, values most likely represent forests before the onset of the epidemic.

Tanoak is one of the tree species that may die after developing trunk lesions from *Phytophthora ramorum*. Tanoak death observed by Marin County homeowners in 1995 was the first indication of the disease (Svihra 2001). Tanoaks are aggressive competitors to the more commercially valuable conifers, and thus are often viewed as a nuisance species. However, tanoak is a very important species for wildlife cover and food. The tanoak forest type was the most common forest type in the 12-county area, exceeding either Douglas-fir or redwood forest, and was estimated at 20 percent of the forest area in the 12 counties (table 19).

Douglas-fir and redwood species are also listed as hosts for the pathogen associated with sudden oak death, *Phytophthora ramorum*. After tanoak, the Douglas-fir and redwood forest types were the next most common in the 12 counties, making up 14 and 13 percent of the forest area respectively (table 19). Most of the other common forest types in the 12 counties (table 19) were also dominated by species that are known hosts to the pathogen, including the coast live oak, California black oak, Pacific madrone, canyon live oak, California laurel, and bigleaf maple forest types. In the 12 counties an estimated 3.8 million acres (±4 percent se), which was 74 percent of the inventoried forest land, was dominated by species (*Acer macrophyllum, Aesculus californica, Arbutus menziesii, Lithocarpus densiflorus, Pseudotsuga menziesii, Quercus agrifolia, Quercus chrysolepis, Quercus kelloggii, Sequoia sempervirens,* and *Umbellularia californica*) that were listed as regulated hosts for the disease as of March 2004.

Tree species seem to differ in their susceptibility to the disease: tanoak, coast live oak, California black oak, and Shreve's oak (*Quercus parvula* var. *shrevei*)[4] are believed to be particularly subject to lethal trunk infections (Rizzo and others 2002). There have been anecdotal reports of mortality in rhododendrons and madrones with the disease (Garbelotto and others 2003). Symptoms observed in the field often appear to be patchy, although the reasons for this are unknown. California laurel, California buckeye, and bigleaf maple appear to have very limited stem infection (Garbelotto and others 2003). Symptoms for overstory Douglas-fir and redwood trees have not been observed, although effects on sprouts and saplings have been reported (Garbelotto and others 2003).

In the 12 counties, the area where tree host species were present was estimated at 4.1 million acres (±3 percent se), which was 81 percent of the estimated forest area for sampled land (table 20). For this estimate, "presence" was determined by the occurrence of at least one host species tree of any size on a subplot. This estimate of occurrence for regulated host species was made from sampled tree data only and would increase if shrub or understory vegetation were included. Nontree host species include toyon, California honeysuckle, rhododendron, wood rose, starflower, California huckleberry, and others.

Two of the acorn-producing species that can die from *Phytophthora ramorum*—tanoak and California black oak—were widely found throughout coniferous timberland forest (Douglas-fir and redwood forest types) and are thus important ecosystem components even in places where they form a relatively small part of the total tree species mix. Raphael (1987) describes numerous wildlife uses of tanoak in northwestern California Douglas-fir forests; salamanders (*Dicamptodon ensatus, Plethodon elongatus, Ensatina eschscholtzi, Aneides flavipunctatus,* and *Aneides ferreus*) using tanoak logs for cover, bears and flying squirrels feeding on tanoak acorns (fig. 19), woodrats using tanoak for nesting, and fishers (*Martes pennanti*) feeding on prey associating with tanoak. Another hardwood tree found in coniferous forests—California black oak—also produces abundant acorn crops in some years, particularly trees older than 80 years

Most major tree species and many shrub species are host for the pathogen causing sudden oak death, but susceptibility and mode of transmission are unknown.

---

[4] *Quercus parvula* is not considered a tree species in these inventories. *Quercus parvula* v. *shrevei* takes tree form and hybridizes with *Q. wislizeni* (Nixon 2002), *Q. agrifolia,* and *Q. kelloggii* (Hickman 1993), so it is possible that it is partially included within estimates for other species.

Figure 19—Tanoak (*Lithocarpus densiflorus*), one of the trees particularly susceptible to sudden oak death, produces abundant acorn crops used by wildlife.

(Tappeiner and McDonald 1980). Pacific madrone is a third hardwood that is a listed host species and common in coniferous coastal forests, and it can also be an important wildlife food source through the production of berries. The three species combined—California black oak, tanoak, and Pacific madrone—are critical components of the coniferous forest, and they can complement each other by differences in timing and amount of acorn, berry, and leaf production. Coast live oak forest, which supplies a half million acres of oak habitat in the quarantined counties, is also subject to lethal trunk lesions from *Phytophthora ramorum*.

At this time, growth and mortality effects of *Phytophthora ramorum* for different plant species are largely unknown, the level of genetic resistance in host species is unknown, the potential range of the disease is unknown, the mode of transmission is unknown, and the environmental factors that lead to susceptibility from the disease are unknown. However, the disease has spread fairly rapidly, albeit patchily, and *Phytophthora ramorum* is now found in a wide geographic area. All but a few of the major tree species in substantial portions of the state are hosts for the disease, as are many of the widespread shrub species. Three of the tree species that appear most susceptible to mortality from *Phytophthora ramorum*— tanoak, coast live oak, and California black oak—were very widespread, predominant for 36 percent of the forest and also found throughout many other forest types. These hardwood species are known to be important as food and habitat for a large number of wildlife species. Although predictions of the long-term effects of the disease are speculative, it appears that there is the potential for very extensive changes in species composition and forest structure over a geographic range encompassing millions of acres of California forest land with the potential for many indirect ecosystem effects, including possible impacts on numerous wildlife species.

Glossary

aboveground biomass—The oven-dry weight of a tree in tons, including the bark, live branches, and total stem (from ground to tree tip).

annual gross growth volume—An annual estimate of the increase in the gross volume of trees during the remeasurement period (1981-84 to 1991-94), for trees that were ≥5 inches d.b.h. in 1994 or ≥5 inches d.b.h. at the time of harvest. Annual growth volume includes ingrowth, growth of survivor trees, and growth of harvested trees.

annual mortality volume—An annual estimate of the gross volume of all trees ≥5 inches d.b.h. that were alive at the previous inventory (1981-84) and died during the remeasurement period (1981-84 to 1991-94). Cull trees were included in this estimate.

annual net growth volume—An annual estimate of net growth for the remeasurement period (1981-84 to 1991-94), calculated as gross growth volume – mortality volume – removal volume. See definitions for mortality and removal volume.

annual removals volume—An annual estimate of the gross volume of all trees ≥5 inches d.b.h. that were alive at the previous inventory (1981-84) and were cut as a result of commercial harvesting, silvicultural activities, or were damaged and killed by logging activities during the remeasurement period (1981-84 to 1991-94). Cull trees were included in this estimate.

average annual precipitation—Annual precipitation in inches, averaged from 1961 to 1990. This was estimated for forest type by combining inventory data with the precipitation GIS theme produced by the Spatial Climate Analysis Service (2004).

basal area—The cross-sectional area of tree stems at 4.5 feet above the ground. Estimates classifying forest into basal area categories will be affected by plot size and condition mapping.

canopy cover (tree)—The percentage of land area covered by the vertical projection of tree crowns.

cull tree—Live trees of noncommercial species, and live trees of commercial species that are more than 75 percent defective because of poor form or rot.

cull trees, rotten—Cull trees that are more than 75 percent defective owing to rot caused by pathogens or other biotic organisms.

cull trees, sound—Trees of noncommercial species or cull trees of commercial species with defect caused primarily by poor form and roughness. Noncommercial hardwood species outside of national forests are Pacific dogwood (*Cornus nuttallii*), walnut (*Juglans* spp.), ailanthus (*Ailanthus altissima*), apple (*Malus* spp.), water birch (*Betula occidentalis*), and willow (*Salix* spp.). Noncommercial hardwood species in national forests include boxelder (*Acer negundo*), walnut, and blue oak.

culturally killed trees—Trees that were killed by human activity but not harvested. Includes trees killed from girdling or from damage by mechanical equipment during logging.

d.b.h. (diameter at breast height)—Diameter outside bark measured at 4.5 feet above the ground.

forest condition—An area of forest that is homogenous in some attributes. When two or more distinct conditions occurred on a plot, the boundaries were mapped and attributes were assigned separately to each. For example, separate conditions could be used for boundaries between forest and nonforest, between hardwood and coniferous forest types, or between uncut and partially harvested areas.

forest land—Land at least 10 percent stocked with live trees, or land that had this minimum tree stocking in the past and is not currently developed for nonforest use. For hardwood forest types in California, at least 10 percent stocked is interpreted as at least 10 percent tree canopy cover. The minimum area recognized is 1 acre.

forest type—Forest type is assigned to conditions by applying a classification algorithm to the field plot data. Forest conditions with more than 50 percent of the stocking in hardwoods are classified as hardwood forest types. The classification process is intended to give results similar to using tree canopy cover, so that the type assigned would be named after the species with the highest amount of cover. See Waddell (1991) for details. Forest type is sensitive to the classification algorithm used, as well as to the plot size and configuration.

gross volume—Volume in cubic feet from the top of a stump 12 inches tall to a minimum 4-inch top (of central stem) inside the bark, with no deductions for sound or rotten cull. This volume is calculated for both cull and noncull trees ≥5 inches d.b.h.

growing-stock volume—Net volume in cubic feet of live sawtimber and poletimber-sized trees (d.b.h. ≥5 inches) excluding cull trees, from the top of a stump 12 inches tall to a minimum 4-inch top (of central stem) inside the bark. Net volume is gross volume less deductions for sound and rotten cull.

other public lands—Lands administered by public agencies other than the USDA Forest Service. Other public lands do not include Native American lands, which are included with private lands.

periodic mortality volume—The gross volume of all trees ≥5 inches d.b.h. that were live at the previous inventory (1984) and died during the remeasurement period (1984 to 1994). Cull trees were included in this estimate.

periodic removals volume—The gross volume of all trees ≥5 inches d.b.h. that were live at the previous inventory (1984) and were cut as a result of commercial harvesting, silvicultural activities, or were damaged and killed by logging activities during the remeasurement period (1984 to 1994). Cull trees were included in this estimate.

regeneration stocking—A classification used to show relative abundance of seedlings and saplings (trees ≤5 inches d.b.h.). On oak woodlands, seedlings were sampled with 16.4-foot-radius subplots and saplings were sampled with 10.8-foot-radius subplots. Stocking estimates are sensitive to the classification method used, as well as to the plot size and configuration.

Nonstocked: no seedlings or saplings on all five subplots

Lightly stocked: one or more seedlings or saplings on one or two of five subplots

Moderately stocked: one or more seedlings or saplings on three or four of five subplots

Well stocked: one or more seedlings or saplings on all five subplots

reserved forest land—For this inventory, reserved forest land was forest land that was dedicated to noncommodity use through statute, ordinance, or administrative order.

resource area—A set of contiguous counties in the state used for inventory scheduling and reporting in the 1980s and 1990s. Resource areas in California are:

Central Coast: Alameda, Contra Costa, Marin, Monterey, San Benito, San Francisco, San Luis Obispo, San Mateo, Santa Barbara, Santa Clara, Santa Cruz, Solano, and Ventura Counties

North Coast: Del Norte, Humboldt, Mendocino, and Sonoma Counties

North Interior: Lassen, Modoc, Shasta, Siskiyou, and Trinity Counties

Sacramento: Butte, Colusa, El Dorado, Glenn, Lake, Napa, Nevada, Placer, Plumas, Sacramento, Sierra, Sutter, Tehama, Yolo, and Yuba Counties

San Joaquin and Southern: Alpine, Amador, Calaveras, Fresno, Imperial, Inyo, Kern, Kings, Los Angeles, Madera, Mariposa, Merced, Mono, Orange, Riverside, San Bernardino, San Diego, San Joaquin, Stanislaus, Tulare, and Tuolumne Counties

sampling error (se)—Sampling error is shown either in the same units as the estimate or as a percentage. The percentage sampling error is calculated as the square root of the estimated variance of the estimate, divided by the estimate itself. A common interpretation of sampling error is that there is a 68-percent chance that the estimate is within the sampling error of the true population value, assuming that estimates are normally distributed, and there is a 95-percent chance that the estimate is within twice the sampling error of the true population value. Tables in this report display values for all cells, even when sampling error is high and there is no meaningful difference among cell values; readers are advised to use the sampling error in interpreting the estimates. Sampling error is displayed as 100 percent for cases with a single observation. For details on how sampling error was calculated for these inventories, please see Barrett (2004).

saplings—Live trees between 1 and 5 inches d.b.h.

savanna—Wildland characterized by widely spaced trees and less than 10 percent total tree canopy cover. For hardwood forests, savanna was not considered forest land.

sawtimber trees—For hardwoods, live trees that are at least 11 inches d.b.h.

seedlings—Live trees less than 1 inch d.b.h.

timberland—Forest land capable of growing 20 cubic feet or more per acre per year (mean annual increment at culmination in fully stocked, natural stands) of industrial wood. Timberland is often referred to as productive forest land. In this report, timberland can be both unreserved and reserved.

total stem volume—The volume of an entire tree bole, from the ground to the tree tip. No volume has been deducted because of rot or poor form.

tree—The determination of what plants are trees is made by species and is specific to an inventory. For these inventories, mountain mahogany, buckthorn (*Rhamnus* spp.), elderberry (*Sambucus* spp.), and rhododendron were not considered trees, but willows were considered trees. A full list of tree species for these inventories can be found in appendix 1.

unproductive forest—Forest land that does not meet the definition of timberland. Unproductive forest is forest that is not capable of producing 20 cubic feet per acre per year at the culmination of mean annual increment.

vegetation, nontree—Understory vegetation is not estimated in this report, but for descriptive purposes we have listed it for common forest types in descending order of occurrence when found at more than 3 plot locations for plots that were entirely within that forest type. Vegetation information came from five 5-meter-radius subplots per plot; where species were unknown, plants are listed as "grass," "forbs," or "shrubs." Common and scientific names for species are shown in appendix 1. Understory vegetation information for national forests is not incorporated into the report.

woodland—Unless otherwise noted, estimates in this report labeled "woodland" include all unproductive hardwood forest. "Oak woodland" refers specifically to unproductive oak forest types.

Acknowledgments

Special thanks to all the landowners who allowed field crews access to their lands to visit plots and measure trees.

Many people were involved in the collection of data, database development, and design of the FIA inventory: Tony Akins, Dale Baer, Shelly Belin, Chris Berger, Steve Bolon, Sarah Butler, Perry Colclasure, Vince Condon, Jim Critchfield, Brian Daum, Pete Delzotto, John Donathon, Paul Dunham, Tim Ferrell, Mariah Fink, Jen Gomoll, Eric Green, Erica Hanson, Jim Harrow, Joanne Hildreth, Bob Hinds, Bruce Hiserote, Eric Johnson, John Kloster, J.D. Lloyd, Doug Magee, Colin MacLean, Michelle Marshall, Neil McKay, Tom Meade, Nick Monkevich, Rich Randle, Jeff Rose, Sarah Phillips, Sam Solano, Janet Steffani, Paul Tufts, Stan Wageman, Mike Weiser, and Karen Williams. Chuck Bolsinger provided the first assessment of California hardwoods and continues to patiently answer questions about FIA inventories.

The help of Ralph Warbington, Deb Beardsley, and other Region 5 personnel in California allowed us to include hardwoods on national forests in this assessment. We thank Rick Standiford, Chuck Bolsinger, Olaf Kuegler, and Bill Stewart for their helpful comments on a draft version of the manuscript.

Metric Equivalents

When you know:	Multiply by:	To find:
Inches	2.54	Centimeters
Feet	.3048	Meters
Miles	1.609	Kilometers
Acres	.405	Hectares
Cubic feet	.0283	Cubic meters
Cubic feet per acre	.06997	Cubic meters per hectare
Square feet	.0929	Square meters
Square feet per acre	.229	Square meters per hectare
Tons per acre	2.24	Megagrams per hectare

Literature Cited

Adams, T.E.; McDougald, N.K. 1995. Planted blue oaks may need help to survive in southern Sierras. California Agriculture. 49(5): 13-17.

Barrett, R.H. 1980. Mammals of California oak habitats—management implications. In: Plumb, T.R., tech. coord. Proceedings of the symposium on the ecology, management, and utilization of California oaks. Gen. Tech. Rep. PSW-GTR-44. Berkeley, CA: U.S. Department of Agriculture, Forest Service, Pacific Southwest Forest and Range Experiment Station: 275-291.

Barrett, T.M. 2004. Estimation procedures for the combined 1990s periodic forest inventories of California, Oregon, and Washington. Gen. Tech. Rep. PNW-GTR-597. Portland, OR: U.S. Department of Agriculture, Forest Service, Pacific Northwest Research Station. 19 p.

Bartolome, J.W.; McClaran, M.P.; Allen-Diaz, B.H.; Dunne, J.; Ford, L.D.; Standiford, R.B.; McDougald, N.K.; Forero, L.C. 2002. Effects of fire and browsing on regeneration of blue oak. In: Standiford, R.B.; McCreary, D.; Purcell, K.L., tech. coords. Proceedings of the fifth symposium on oak woodlands: oaks in California's changing landscape. Gen. Tech. Rep. PSW-GTR-126. Albany, CA: U.S. Department of Agriculture, Forest Service, Pacific Southwest Research Station: 281-286.

Bolsinger, C.L. 1988. The hardwoods of California's timberlands, woodlands, and savannas. Resour. Bull. PNW-RB-148. Portland, OR: U.S. Department of Agriculture, Forest Service, Pacific Northwest Research Station. 148 p.

Borchert, M.I.; Davis, F.W.; Michaelsen, J.; Oyler, L.D. 1989. Interactions of factors affecting seedling recruitment of blue oak (*Quercus douglasii*) in California. Ecology. 70(2): 389-404.

Bowyer, R.T.; Bleich, V.C. 1980. Ecological relationships between southern mule deer and California black oak. In: Plumb, T.R., tech. coord. Proceedings of the symposium on the ecology, management, and utilization of California oaks. Gen. Tech. Rep. PSW-GTR-44. Berkeley, CA: U.S. Department of Agriculture, Forest Service, Pacific Southwest Forest and Range Experiment Station: 292-296.

Brackett, M. 1973. Notes on tariff tree volume computation. DNR report 24. Olympia, WA: Washington Department of Natural Resources. 26 p.

California Department of Fish and Game [CDFG]. 2002. CWHR version 8.0 personal computer program. Sacramento, CA: California Interagency Wildlife Task Group.

California Department of Forestry and Fire Protection [CDFFP]. 2003. The changing California: forest and range 2003 assessment, assessment summary. Sacramento, CA. 228 p.

Delfino, K.L. 1986. California's hardwoods—what potential? In: Plumb, T.R.; Pillsbury, N.H., coords. Proceedings of the symposium on multiple-use management of California's hardwood resources. Gen. Tech. Rep. PSW-GTR-100. Berkeley, CA: U.S. Department of Agriculture, Forest Service, Pacific Southwest Forest and Range Experiment Station: 286-288.

Fried, J.S.; Bolsinger, C.L.; Beardsley, D. 2004. Chaparrral in southern and central coastal California in the mid-1990s: area, ownership, condition, and change. Gen. Tech. Rep. PNW-RB-240. Portland, OR: U.S. Department of Agriculture, Forest Service, Pacific Northwest Research Station. 86 p.

Garbelotto, M.; Davidson, J.M.; Ivors, K.; Maloney, P.E.; Huberli, D; Koike, S.T.; Rizzo, D.M. 2003. Non-oak native plants are main hosts for sudden oak death pathogen in California. California Agriculture. 57(1): 18-23.

Hall, L.M.; George, M.R.; McCreary, D.D.; Adams, T.E. 1992. Effects of cattle grazing on blue oak seedling damage and survival. Journal of Range Management. 45: 503-506.

Hickman, J.C., ed. 1993. The Jepson manual: higher plants of California. Berkeley, CA: University of California Press. 1,400 p.

Horney, M.; Standiford, R.B., McCreary, D.; Tecklin, J.; Richards, R. 2002. Effects of wildfire on blue oak in the Sacramento Valley. In: Standiford, R.B.; McCreary, D.; Purcell, K.L., tech. coords. Proceedings of the fifth symposium on oak woodlands: oaks in California's changing landscape. Gen. Tech. Rep. PSW-GTR-126. Albany, CA: U.S. Department of Agriculture, Forest Service, Pacific Southwest Research Station: 261-267.

Huber, D.W.; McDonald, P.M. 1992. California's hardwood resource: history and reasons for lack of a sustained hardwood industry. Gen. Tech. Rep. PSW-GTR-135. Albany, CA: U.S. Department of Agriculture, Forest Service, Pacific Southwest Research Station. 14 p.

Huntsinger, L.; Buttolph, L; Hopkinson, P. 1997. Ownership and management changes on California hardwood rangelands: 1985 to 1992. Journal of Range Management. 50(4): 423-430.

Huntsinger, L; Fortmann, L.P. 1990. California's privately owned oak woodlands: owners, use, and management. Journal of Range Management. 43(2): 147-152.

Kelly, M.; Meentemeyer, R.K. 2002. Landscape dynamics of the spread of sudden oak death. Photogrammetric Engineering and Remote Sensing. 68(10): 1001-1009.

Koenig, W.D.; McCullough, D.R.; Vaughn, C.E; Knops, J.M.H.; Carmen, W.J. 1999. Synchrony and asynchrony of acorn production at two coastal California sites. Madroño. 46(1): 20-24.

Light, R.H; Pedroni, L.E. 2002. When oak ordinances fail: unaddressed issues of oak conservation. In: Standiford, R.B.; McCreary, D.; Purcell, K.L., tech. coords. Proceedings of the fifth symposium on oak woodlands: oaks in California's changing landscape. Gen. Tech. Rep. PSW-GTR-126. Albany, CA: U.S. Department of Agriculture, Forest Service, Pacific Southwest Research Station: 483-500.

McClaran, M.P.; Bartolome, J.W. 1989. Fire-related recruitment in stagnant *Quercus douglasii* populations. Canadian Journal of Forest Research. 19(5): 580-585.

McDonald, P.M.; Tappeiner, J.C. 2002. California's hardwood resource: seeds, seedlings, and sprouts of three important forest-zone species. Gen. Tech. Rep. PSW-GTR-185. Albany, CA: U.S. Department of Agriculture, Forest Service, Pacific Southwest Research Station. 39 p.

McPherson, B.A.; Wood, D.L.; Storer, A.J.; Kelly, N.M.; Standiford, R.B. 2002. Sudden oak death: disease trends in Marin County plots after one year. In: Standiford, R.B.; McCreary, D.; Purcell, K.L., tech. coords. Proceedings of the fifth symposium on oak woodlands: oaks in California's changing landscape. Gen. Tech. Rep. PSW-GTR-126. Albany, CA: U.S. Department of Agriculture, Forest Service, Pacific Southwest Research Station: 751-764.

Mensing, S.A. 1992. The impact of European settlement on blue oak (*Quercus douglasii*) regeneration and recruitment in the Tehachapi Mountains, California. Madroño. 39(1): 36-46.

Morgan, T.A.; Keegan, C.E., III; Dillon, T.; Chase, A.L.; Fried, J.S.; Weber, M.N. 2004. California's forest products industry: a descriptive analysis. Gen. Tech. Rep. PNW-GTR-615. Portland, OR: U.S. Department of Agriculture, Forest Service, Pacific Northwest Research Station. 55 p.

Muick, P.C.; Bartolome, J.R. 1987. An assessment of natural regeneration of oaks in California; final report with supplement. Sacramento, CA: California Department of Forestry, Forest and Rangeland Resource Assessment Program. 115 p.

Munz, P.A.; Keck, D.D. 1959. A California flora and supplement. Berkeley, CA: University of California Press. 1,905 p.

Nixon, K.C. 2002. The oak (*Quercus*) biodiversity of California and adjacent regions. In: Standiford, R.B.; McCreary, D.; Purcell, K.L., tech. coords. Proceedings of the fifth symposium on oak woodlands: oaks in California's changing landscape. Gen. Tech. Rep. PSW-GTR-126. Albany, CA: U.S. Department of Agriculture, Forest Service, Pacific Southwest Research Station: 3-20.

Pillsbury, N.H; Kirkley, M.L. 1984. Equations for total, wood, and saw-log volume for thirteen California hardwoods. Res. Note PNW-414. Portland, OR: U.S. Department of Agriculture, Forest Service, Pacific Northwest Forest and Range Experiment Station. 52 p.

Pillsbury, N.H.; Verner, J.; Tietje, W.D., tech. coords. 1997. Proceedings of a symposium on oak woodlands: ecology, management, and urban interface issues. Gen. Tech. Rep. PSW-GTR-160. Albany, CA: U.S. Department of Agriculture, Forest Service, Pacific Southwest Research Station. 738 p.

Plumb, T.R., tech. coord. 1980. Proceedings of the symposium on the ecology, management, and utilization of California oaks. Gen. Tech. Rep. PSW-GTR-44. Berkeley, CA: U.S. Department of Agriculture, Forest Service, Pacific Southwest Forest and Range Experiment Station. 368 p.

Plumb, T.R.; Pillsbury, N.H., tech. coords. 1987. Proceedings of the symposium on multiple-use management of California's hardwood resources. Gen. Tech. Rep. PSW-GTR-100. Berkeley, CA: U.S. Department of Agriculture, Forest Service, Pacific Southwest Forest and Range Experiment Station. 462 p.

Raphael, M.G. 1987. Wildlife-tanoak associations in Douglas-fir forests of northwestern California. In: Plumb, T.R.; Pillsbury, N.H., tech. coords. Proceedings of the symposium on multiple-use management of California's hardwood resources. Gen. Tech. Rep. PSW-GTR-100. Berkeley, CA: U.S. Department of Agriculture, Forest Service, Pacific Southwest Forest and Range Experiment Station: 183-189.

Rizzo, D.M.; Garbelotto, M. 2003. Sudden oak death: endangering California and Oregon forest ecosystems. Frontiers in Ecology and the Environment. 1(5): 197-204.

Rizzo, D.M.; Garbelotto, M.; Davidson, J.M.; Slaughter, G.W.; Koike, S.T. 2002. *Phytophthora ramorum* as the cause of extensive mortality of *Quercus* spp. and *Lithocarpus densiflorus* in California. Plant Disease. 86(3): 205-214.

Spatial Climate Analysis Service. 2004. California average annual precipitation 1961-90 [Vector GIS theme]. Corvallis, OR: Oregon State University. http://www.ocs.orst.edu/prism/index.phtml. (20 January).

Standiford, R.B., tech. coord. 1991. Proceedings of the symposium on oak woodlands and hardwood rangeland management. Gen. Tech. Rep. PSW-GTR-126. Albany, CA: U.S. Department of Agriculture, Forest Service, Pacific Southwest Research Station. 376 p.

Standiford, R.B. 2001. California oak woodlands. In: McShea, W.J.; Healy, W.M., eds. Oak forest ecosystems: ecology and management for wildlife. Baltimore, MD: The Johns Hopkins University Press: 280-303.

Standiford, R.B.; McCreary, D.; Purcell, K.L., tech. coords. 2002. Proceedings of the fifth symposium on oak woodlands: oaks in California's changing landscape. Gen. Tech. Rep. PSW-GTR-126. Albany, CA: U.S. Department of Agriculture, Forest Service, Pacific Southwest Research Station. 846 p.

Standiford, R.; McDougald, N.; Frost, W.; Phillips, R. 1997. Factors influencing the probability of oak regeneration on southern Sierra Nevada woodlands in California. Madroño. 44(2): 170-183.

Sudworth, G.B. 1908. Forest trees of the Pacific slope. Washington, DC: U.S. Department of Agriculture, Forest Service. 441 p.

Svihra, P. 2001. Diagnosis of SOD: case study of a scientific process. California Agriculture. 55(1): 12-14.

Swiecki, T.J.; Bernhardt, E. 2002. Effects of fire on naturally occurring blue oak (*Quercus douglasii*) saplings. In: Standiford, R.B.; McCreary, D.; Purcell, K.L., tech. coords. Proceedings of the fifth symposium on oak woodlands: oaks in California's changing landscape. Gen. Tech. Rep. PSW-GTR-126. Albany, CA: U.S. Department of Agriculture, Forest Service, Pacific Southwest Research Station: 251-259.

Swiecki, T.J.; Bernhardt, E.; Drake, C. 1997. Factors affecting blue oak sapling recruitment. In: Pillsbury, N.H.; Verner, J.; Tietje, W.D., tech. coords. Proceedings of a symposium on oak woodlands: ecology, management, and urban interface issues. Gen. Tech. Rep. PSW-GTR-160. Albany, CA: U.S. Department of Agriculture, Forest Service, Pacific Southwest Research Station: 157-167.

Tappeiner, J.; McDonald, P. 1980. Preliminary recommendations for managing California black oak in the Sierra Nevada. In: Plumb, T.R., tech. coord. Proceedings of the symposium on the ecology, management, and utilization of California oaks. Gen. Tech. Rep. PSW-GTR-44. Berkeley, CA: U.S. Department of Agriculture, Forest Service, Pacific Southwest Forest and Range Experiment Station: 107-111.

Tietje, W.D.; Waddell, K.L.; Vreeland, J.K.; Bolsinger, C.L. 2002. Coarse woody debris in oak woodlands in California. Western Journal of Applied Forestry. 17(3): 139-146.

Urban Forest Ecosystems Institute [UFEI]. 2004. California registry of big trees. http://www.ufei.org/BigTrees/index.html. (02 January).

U.S. Department of Commerce, Bureau of the Census. 2004. Census 2000, summary for California. http://factfinder.census.gov. (03 March).

Verner, J. 1980. Birds of California oak habitats—management implications. In: Plumb, T.R., tech. coord. Proceedings of the symposium on the ecology, management, and utilization of California oaks. Gen. Tech. Rep. PSW-GTR-44. Berkeley, CA: U.S. Department of Agriculture, Forest Service, Pacific Southwest Forest and Range Experiment Station: 246-264.

Waddell, K.L. 1991. California inventory, procedures and techniques reference documentation. 177 p. Unpublished document. On file with: PNW-FIA, P.O. Box 3890, Portland, OR 97208.

Waddell, K.L.; Bassett, P.M. 1996. Timber resource statistics for the North Coast Resource Area of California, 1994. Resour. Bull. PNW-RB-214. Portland, OR: U.S. Department of Agriculture, Forest Service, Pacific Northwest Research Station. 50 p.

Waddell, K.L.; Bassett, P.M. 1997a. Timber resource statistics for the Central Coast Resource Area of California, 1994. Resour. Bull. PNW-RB-221. Portland, OR: U.S. Department of Agriculture, Forest Service, Pacific Northwest Research Station. 45 p.

Waddell, K.L.; Bassett, P.M. 1997b. Timber resource statistics for the Sacramento Resource Area of California. Resour. Bull. PNW-RB-220. Portland, OR: U.S. Department of Agriculture, Forest Service, Pacific Northwest Research Station. 50 p.

Appendix 1. Scientific and Common Plant Names

Scientific name[a]	Common name

Trees

Ailanthus altissima (Miller) Swingle	ailanthus
Malus L. spp.	apple
Pseudotsuga macrocarpa (Vasey) Mayr	bigcone Douglas-fir
Acer macrophyllum Pursh	bigleaf maple
Pinus muricata D. Don	Bishop pine
Populus balsamifera L. ssp. *trichocarpa* Torrey & A. Gray	black cottonwood
Quercus douglasii Hook. & Arn.	blue oak
Acer negundo L. var. *californicum* (Torry & A. Gray) Sarg.	boxelder
Quercus kelloggii Newb.	California black oak
Aesculus californica (Spach) Nutt.	California buckeye
Juniperus californica Carrière	California juniper
Umbellularia californica (Hook. & Arn.) Nutt.	California laurel, bay laurel
Torreya californica Torrey	California nutmeg, California torrey
Platanus racemosa Nutt.	California sycamore
Quercus chrysolepis Liebm.	canyon live oak
Quercus agrifolia Nee	coast live oak
Pinus coulteri D. Don	Coulter pine
Pseudotsuga menziesii (Mirbel) Franco	Douglas-fir
Quercus engelmannii E. Greene	Engelmann oak
Eucalyptus L'Her. spp.	eucalyptus
Pinus sabiniana Douglas	ghost pine, gray pine, foothill pine
Castanopsis chrysophylla (Hook.) Hjelmq.	giant chinquapin, golden chinkapin
Sequoiadendron giganteum (Lindley) Buchholz	giant sequoia
Calocedrus decurrens (Torry) Florin	incense cedar
Quercus wislizeni A.DC.	interior live oak
Pinus jeffreyi Grev. & Balf.	Jeffrey pine
Pinus attenuata Lemmon	knobcone pine
Fraxinus latifolia Benth.	Oregon ash
Quercus garryana Hook.	Oregon white oak
Cornus nuttallii Audubon	Pacific dogwood
Arbutus menziesii Pursh	Pacific madrone
Pinus ponderosa Laws.	ponderosa pine
Populus tremuloides Michaux	quaking aspen
Alnus rubra Bong.	red alder
Sequoia sempervirens (D. Don) Endl.	redwood, coastal redwood
Pinus lambertiana Dougl.	sugar pine
Lithocarpus densiflorus (Hook. & Arn.) Rehder	tanoak

Scientific name[a]	Common name
Quercus lobata Nee	valley oak, California white oak
Juglans L. spp.	walnut
Betula occidentalis Hook.	water birch
Alnus rhombifolia Nutt.	white alder
Abies concolor (Gordon & Glend.) Lindley	white fir
Salix L. spp.	willow

Nontree vegetation

Baccharis L. spp.	baccharis
Chamaebatia foliolosa Benth.	bear-clover
Ceanothus thyrsiflorus Eschsch.	blueblossom ceanothus
Ceanothus cuneatus (Hook.) Nutt.	buckbrush
Rhamnus L. spp.	buckthorn
Corylus cornuta var. *californica* (A. DC.) Sharp	California hazelnut
Lonicera hispidula Dougl.	California honeysuckle
Vaccinium ovatum Pursh	California huckleberry
Torreya californica Torrey	California nutmeg
Cercis occidentalis Torrey	California redbud
Quercus dumosa Nutt.	California scrub oak
Rhododendron macrophyllum D. Don	coast rhododendron
Ceanothus incanus Torrey & A. Gray	coast whitethorn
Arctostaphylos manzanita C. Parry	common manzanita
Ceanothus integerrimus Hook. & Arn.	deerbrush
Sambucus L. spp.	elderberry
Galium triflorum Michx.	fragrant bedstraw
Gramineae spp.	grass
Arctostaphylos patula E. Greene	greenleaf manzanita
Arctostaphylos columbiana Piper	hairy manzanita
Rhamnus ilicifolia Kellogg	hollyleaf redberry
Iris L. spp.	iris
Claytonia perfoliata Willd.	miner's lettuce
Cercocarpus betuloides Torrey & A. Gray	mountain mahogany
Berberis aquifolium Pursh	mountain-grape
Avena L. spp.	oats
Myrica californica Cham. & Schldl.	Pacific wax-myrtle
Toxicodendron diversilobum (Torr. & Gray) Greene	poison oak
Vaccinium parvifolium Smith	red huckleberry
Erodium cicutarium (L.) L'Hèr	red-stem filaree
Oxalis oregana Nutt.	redwood sorrel
Rhododendron macrophyllum D. Don ex G. Don	rhododendron

Scientific name[a]	Common name
Gaultheria shallon Pursh	salal
Quercus parvula var. *shrevei* (C.H. Muller) K. Nixon[b]	Shreve's oak
Aira caryophyllea L.	silver hairgrass
Symphoricarpos sp. Duham.	snowberry
Trientalis latifolia Hook.	starflower
Arctostaphylos viscida C. Parry	sticky whiteleaf manzanita
Rubus parviflorus Nutt.	thimbleberry
Heteromeles arbutifolia (Lindl.) M. Roemer	toyon
Pteridium aquilinum (L.) Kuhn	western brackenfern
Polystichum munitum (Kaulfuss) K. Presl	western swordfern
Whipplea modesta Torrey	whipplea
Rubus leucodermis Dougl. ex Torr. & Gray	whitebark raspberry
Rosa gymnocarpa Nutt.	wood rose

[a] We are using Hickman (1993) for scientific names. Munz and Keck (1959) was a primary reference source during the planning and field collection for Forest Inventory and Analysis inventories during the 1980s and 1990s.

[b] *Quercus parvula* is not considered a tree species in these inventories. *Quercus parvula* v. *shrevei* takes tree form and hybridizes with *Q. wislizeni* (Nixon 2002), *Q. agrifolia*, and *Q. kelloggii* (Hickman 1993), so it is possible that it is partially included within estimates for other species.

Appendix 2. Inventory Procedures

Outside of national forests and reserved lands, two Forest Inventory and Analysis (FIA) inventories were used to collect information on hardwoods and hardwood forests. The first was an inventory of timberland that used a sampling intensity of one field plot per every 7,400 acres. The second was an inventory of woodland that used one field plot per 14,800 acres. Both inventories used the same field protocols, plot configuration, and analytical procedures such as volume equations and forest typing algorithms. Plots were located by superimposing a grid over the land and randomly locating plots within each grid cell; plots are treated as a random sample for analysis. Field measurements began in 1991 and were completed in 1994.

Plots used for field visits are a subset of plots established and interpreted on air photos. Air photos are used for double sampling for stratification, which improves the precision of estimates. Stratification for results reported here used air photos taken before the 1980s inventory, with the exception of the stratification for the north coast region, which used air photos taken before the 1990s inventory. All field plots also had recent air photos that were used by the field crew in navigating to the plot. Overall, there were 4,824 field plots in California, 2,245 of which fell at least partially in forest land, and 78,223 photointerpreted plots used for stratification. There were 2,412 field plots on the woodland field grid in California, and woodland trees were measured on 540 of these field plots.

Each plot consisted of a cluster of five subplots, with one central subplot, three subplots at 210 feet away to the north, east, and west, and one subplot 141 feet away to the south. On each subplot, trees between 6.9 and 35.5 inches diameter at breast height (d.b.h.) were selected with variable-radius sampling by using a Basal Area Factor (BAF) 30.5 prism (BAF 7 metric prism). Trees greater than 35.7 inches d.b.h. were sampled by using a fixed radius of 55.8 feet. Trees smaller than 6.9 inches were sampled by using a 10.8-ft fixed radius.

When two or more distinct conditions existed on a plot–areas different by broad forest type, size of trees, stocking density, or cutting history—the areas were mapped on the subplots, and the resulting mapped areas used in calculating attributes. In the previous 1980s inventory of California forests, plots were shifted so that they fell in a single condition. In addition, in the 1980s, a three-subplot configuration was used in woodlands rather than a five-subplot configuration, and woodland plots were sampled at a reduced intensity of one plot per 29,600 acres. The net result is that the calculation of 1990s estimates was straightforward, but the calculation of change between 1980 and 1990 was complicated and in some cases involved modeling of tree attributes such as diameter and height.

Most national forest data came from a Pacific Southwest Region inventory conducted in 1993-2000. The underlying base grid for plot selection was the same as for the FIA inventories. However, remote sensing data were used to stratify the area, with classification into broad vegetation types. Plots were sampled with increased intensity for some vegetation types. Because of this intensification, estimates for national forests often have greater precision than estimates for private or other public lands.

The national forest inventory used a five-subplot configuration similar to that of FIA, with subplots spaced at 127 feet from the central subplot. Trees between 1 and 4.9 inches d.b.h. were sampled within an 11.8-ft fixed radius of subplot center. Trees of 5 inches d.b.h. or greater were sampled with either a BAF 20 or BAF 40 prism. If a BAF 20 prism was used, trees 30.4 inches d.b.h. and larger were sampled with a 58.9-foot fixed radius. If a BAF 40 prism was used, trees 42.9 inches d.b.h. and larger were sampled with a 58.9-foot fixed radius. Volume equations and forest typing algorithms used were the same as for FIA. Subplots were assigned to different conditions, but individual subplots were not mapped by condition.

A very small number of plots from the Rogue River and Siskiyou National Forests (Pacific Northwest Region) were also used in the hardwoods assessment. Plots were sampled from a fixed 3.4- or 1.7-mile grid, depending on whether or not they were located in wilderness. As with the other inventories, the plot contained five subplots, but they were located 133.9 feet from the central subplot's center. Trees less than 5 inches d.b.h. were sampled within an 11.8-foot fixed radius of subplot center. Trees between 5 and 12.9 inches were sampled with a 24-foot fixed radius, and trees between 13 and 31.9 inches d.b.h. (east side) or 13 and 47.9 inches d.b.h. (west side) were sampled with a 51.1-foot radius. The largest trees were sampled within a 185.1-foot radius from the central subplot's center. Conditions were not mapped in the field. Forest typing algorithms and volume equation assignments were identical to the FIA inventories.

Volume equations for oaks and most other California hardwoods come from Pillsbury and Kirkley (1984). Volume equations for alder, aspen, and cottonwood come from Brackett (1973). Forest typing was done by a two-step process. If the stocking in hardwood trees was greater than the stocking in coniferous trees, the area would be classed as a hardwood forest type. Then the area would be assigned a specific hardwood forest type according to which hardwood tree species had the greatest stocking. These inventory procedures have been kept consistent with other reports from the 1990s inventories (for example, Waddell and Bassett 1996, 1997a,

1997b). Statistical procedures are described in Barrett (2004). Owing to lack of space, sampling errors are not included for every estimate in the tables, but these can be obtained from the authors upon request.

Although ownership information and plot locations are confidential, other data used in developing this report are available to the public. The four inventories described here have been combined with other inventories into a single database. To request a copy of this "PNW-FIA Integrated Database," please visit the Web site http://www.fs.fed.us/pnw/fia.

Monitoring and assessment of California hardwoods and oak woodlands are continuing. Beginning in 2001, a new forest inventory system was implemented that includes all land in California, both public and private, and both reserved and unreserved forest. One-tenth of all plots are being sampled each year. Over a decade, sampling intensity on woodland will increase to about one plot per 6,000 acres as compared to the one plot per 14,800 acres (current estimates) and one plot per 29,600 acres (change estimates) used in this report. More information on this annual Forest Inventory and Analysis system is available at http://www.fia.fs.fed.us/.

Table 1—Area of hardwood and softwood forest types on woodland and timberland by resource area and reserve status, California, 1990s

Resource area and forest type group	Timberland				Woodland				Total			
	Unreserved	Reserved	Total Area	Total SE %	Unreserved	Reserved	Total Area	Total SE %	Unreserved	Reserved	Total Area	Total SE %
	- - - - Thousand acres - - - -			%	- - - - Thousand acres - - - -			%	- - - - Thousand acres - - - -			%
North Coast:												
Hardwoods	1,831.6	33.2	1,864.9	4	534.8	6.3	541.1	7	2,366.4	39.5	2,406.0	4
Softwoods	1,497.5	140.9	1,638.4	5	3.8	—	3.8	65	1,501.3	140.9	1,642.2	5
Other^a	69.1	12.2	81.3	27	6.9	—	6.9	79	76.0	12.2	88.2	26
Total	3,398.2	186.4	3,584.6	2	545.5	6.3	551.8	7	3,943.7	192.7	4,136.4	2
SE (%)	2	14	2		7	100	7		2	14	2	
North Interior:												
Hardwoods	790.9	89.5	880.4	8	714.2	32.2	746.4	6	1,505.1	121.7	1,626.8	5
Softwoods	5,160.5	633.7	5,794.2	2	227.8	37.5	265.3	15	5,388.3	671.2	6,059.5	2
Other^a	334.6	73.4	408.1	11	76.2	33.5	109.7	30	410.8	106.9	517.8	10
Total	6,286.0	796.6	7,082.6	1	1,018.2	103.2	1,121.4	5	7,304.2	899.8	8,204.0	1
SE (%)	1	8	1		6	29	5		1	7	1	
Sacramento:												
Hardwoods	580.3	26.9	607.2	9	1,605.8	23.1	1,628.9	4	2,186.1	50.0	2,236.1	4
Softwoods	3,744.6	126.7	3,871.3	2	42.1	16.8	58.9	35	3,786.7	143.5	3,930.2	2
Other^a	259.0	24.9	283.9	14	40.6	30.6	71.2	28	299.6	55.5	355.1	12
Total	4,583.8	178.5	4,762.3	1	1,688.5	70.5	1,759.0	4	6,272.3	249.0	6,521.3	1
SE (%)	1	17	1		4	32	4		1	15	1	
Central Coast:												
Hardwoods	157.6	34.8	192.3	15	1,503.8	131.5	1,635.3	5	1,661.4	166.3	1,827.6	5
Softwoods	137.4	55.2	192.5	16	7.0	0.0	7.0	100	144.4	55.2	199.5	16
Other^a	13.0	28.7	41.6	36	47.7	49.6	97.3	25	60.7	78.3	138.9	20
Total	307.9	118.6	426.5	8	1,558.5	181.1	1,739.6	5	1,866.4	299.7	2,166.1	4
SE (%)	9	18			5	19			4	13		

Table 1—Area of hardwood and softwood forest types on woodland and timberland by resource area and reserve status, California, 1990s (continued)

Resource area and forest type group	Timberland				Woodland				Total			
	Unreserved	Reserved	Total Area	SE %	Unreserved	Reserved	Total Area	SE %	Unreserved	Reserved	Total Area	SE %
	– – – – – Thousand acres – – – – –				– – – – Thousand acres – – – –				– – – – Thousand acres – – – –			
Southern:												
Hardwoods	428.3	101.1	529.4	9	2,530.2	134.6	2,664.8	3	2,958.5	235.7	3,194.2	3
Softwoods	1,812.5	977.5	2,790.0	2	189.4	129.4	318.8	17	2,001.9	1,106.9	3,108.8	3
Other[a]	153.0	122.8	275.8	14	343.5	162.3	505.8	12	496.5	285.1	781.6	9
Total	2,393.9	1,201.4	3,595.3		3,063.1	426.3	3,489.4		5,457.0	1,627.7	7,084.7	
SE (%)	3	5	2		3	13	3		2	5	2	
Total, California:												
Hardwoods	3,788.7	285.5	4,074.2	3	6,888.8	327.7	7,216.5	2	10,677.5	613.2	11,290.7	2
Softwoods	12,352.5	1,933.9	14,286.4	1	470.1	183.7	653.8	11	12,822.6	2,117.6	14,940.2	1
Other[a]	828.7	262.1	1,090.7	7	514.9	276.0	790.9	10	1,343.6	538.1	1,881.6	6
Total	16,969.8	2,481.5	19,451.3		7,873.8	787.4	8,661.2		24,843.6	3,268.9	28,112.5	
SE (%)	1	4	1		2	9	2		1	3	1	

Note: Excludes reserved lands outside of national forests because these areas were not sampled.

SE = sampling error.

— = less than 50 acres.

[a] Other includes nonstocked and unclassified types.

Table 2—Area of hardwood forest types on woodland and timberland by resource area and owner, California, 1990s

Resource area and forest type	Woodland					Timberland					Total				
	National forest	Other public	Private	Total Area	SE	National forest	Other public	Private	Total Area	SE	National forest	Other public	Private	Total Area	SE
	Thousand acres				%	Thousand acres				%	Thousand acres				%
North Coast:															
Oak group—[a]															
Blue oak	—	—	29.0	29.0	63	—	—	—	—		—	—	29.0	29.0	63
California black oak	10.1	—	45.3	55.4	43	12.7	1.1	131.0	144.7	20	22.8	1.1	176.3	200.1	19
Canyon live oak	27.4	—	29.1	56.5	43	14.0	23.8	84.4	122.2	23	41.4	23.8	113.5	178.7	21
Coast live oak	—	11.9	85.2	97.1	29	—	—	23.8	23.8	46	—	11.9	109.0	120.9	25
Interior live oak	5.2	—	—	5.2	100	—	1.9	12.3	14.2	63	5.2	1.9	12.3	19.4	53
Oregon white oak	31.8	2.3	133.0	167.2	24	—	—	126.1	126.1	21	31.8	2.3	259.1	293.2	17
Valley oak	—	—	40.3	40.3	57	—	—	13.2	13.2	62	—	—	53.5	53.5	47
Total	74.5	14.2	362.0	450.7		26.7	26.8	390.8	444.2		101.2	41.0	752.8	894.9	
Non-oak group—															
Bigleaf maple	—	—	9.1	9.1	100	—	—	22.0	22.0	58	—	—	31.1	31.1	51
Buckeye	—	—	4.3	4.3	100	—	—	—	—		—	—	4.3	4.3	100
California laurel	—	—	27.0	27.0	68	2.0	—	74.7	76.7	27	2.0	—	101.7	103.7	27
Cottonwood/aspen	—	—	—	—		—	—	5.2	5.2	100	—	—	5.2	5.2	100
Eucalyptus	—	—	—	—		—	—	3.6	3.6	100	—	—	3.6	3.6	100
Giant chinquapin	—	—	—	—		6.6	—	6.2	12.8	59	6.6	—	6.2	12.8	59
Oregon ash	—	—	16.5	16.5	100	—	—	—	—		—	—	16.5	16.5	100
Pacific madrone	—	—	29.5	29.5	70	18.7	11.4	124.9	155.0	21	18.7	11.4	154.4	184.5	22
Red alder	4.1	—	—	4.1	100	2.1	—	75.8	77.9	30	6.2	—	75.8	82.0	29
Tanoak	—	—	—	—		131.2	—	926.8	1,058.0	7	131.2	—	926.8	1,058.0	7
Willow	—	—	—	—		—	—	9.6	9.6	71	—	—	9.6	9.6	71
Total	4.1	—	86.4	90.5		160.6	11.4	1,248.8	1,420.8		164.7	11.4	1,335.2	1,511.3	
Total, North Coast	78.6	14.2	448.4	541.2		187.3	38.2	1,639.6	1,865.0		265.9	52.4	2,088.0	2,406.3	
SE for total (%)	26	45	8	7		15	46	5	4		13	34	4	4	

Table 2—Area of hardwood forest types on woodland and timberland by resource area and owner, California, 1990s (continued)

Resource area and forest type	Woodland					Timberland					Total				
	National forest	Other public	Private	Total Area	Total SE %	National forest	Other public	Private	Total Area	Total SE %	National forest	Other public	Private	Total Area	Total SE %
	Thousand acres				%	*Thousand acres*				%	*Thousand acres*				%
North Interior:															
Oak group—															
Blue oak[a]	15.8	24.6	221.6	262.0	18	—	—	—	—		15.8	24.6	221.6	262.0	18
California black oak	26.2	—	37.5	63.7	40	105.4	8.7	148.1	262.2	15	131.6	8.7	185.6	326.0	14
Canyon live oak	113.7	9.3	34.1	157.2	20	166.3	9.6	75.2	251.2	16	280.0	18.9	109.4	408.3	13
Interior live oak	6.2	—	29.3	35.5	61	12.2	—	—	12.2	60	18.4	—	29.3	47.7	48
Oregon white oak	46.2	26.0	113.5	185.7	21	29.6	9.2	35.2	74.0	28	75.8	35.2	148.7	259.7	17
Valley oak	—	—	17.5	17.5	93	8.0	—	—	8.0	100	8.0	—	17.5	25.5	71
Total	208.1	59.9	453.6	721.7		321.5	27.6	258.5	607.6		529.6	87.5	712.2	1,329.3	
Non-oak group—															
Bigleaf maple	5.7	—	—	5.7	100	12.4	3.4	9.6	25.4	53	18.1	3.4	9.6	31.1	47
California laurel	—	—	—	—		—	—	9.6	9.6	100	—	—	9.6	9.6	100
Cottonwood/aspen	—	—	7.2	7.2	100	20.6	1.7	—	22.3	48	20.6	1.7	7.2	29.5	44
Dogwood	—	—	—	—		—	—	3.2	3.2	100	—	—	3.2	3.2	100
Giant chinquapin	—	—	—	—		11.6	—	—	11.6	98	11.6	—	—	11.6	98
Pacific madrone	9.3	—	—	9.3	100	57.0	—	22.5	79.5	29	66.3	—	22.5	88.8	28
Red alder	—	—	—	—		10.4	—	—	10.4	82	10.4	—	—	10.4	82
Tanoak	2.6	—	—	2.6	100	87.0	—	23.7	110.7	24	89.6	—	23.7	113.3	24
Total	17.6	—	7.2	24.8		199.0	5.1	68.6	272.7		216.6	5.1	75.8	297.5	
Total, North Interior	225.7	59.9	460.9	746.5	6	520.5	32.7	327.1	880.3	8	746.2	92.6	788.0	1,626.8	5
SE for total (%)	13	22	7	6		10	43	14	8		8	22	7	5	

Table 2—Area of hardwood forest types on woodland and timberland by resource area and owner, California, 1990s (continued)

Resource area and forest type	Woodland					Timberland					Total				
	National forest	Other public	Private	Total Area	Total SE %	National forest	Other public	Private	Total Area	Total SE %	National forest	Other public	Private	Total Area	Total SE %
	Thousand acres				%	*Thousand acres*				%	*Thousand acres*				%
Sacramento:															
Oak group—															
Blue oak[a]	1.4	35.8	992.0	1,029.2	8	—	—	—	—		87.1	35.8	992.0	1,029.2	8
California black oak	36.6	—	60.1	96.7	29	164.4	—	149.1	313.5	13	201.0	—	209.2	410.2	12
Canyon live oak	118.6	21.0	76.2	215.8	19	85.7	19.7	73.9	179.3	18	204.3	40.7	150.1	395.1	13
Interior live oak	7.4	—	243.3	250.7	21	3.5	—	33.7	37.2	40	10.9	—	277.0	287.9	19
Oregon white oak	8.4	—	—	8.4	100	—	—	—	—		8.4	—	—	8.4	100
Valley oak	1.4	—	17.5	18.9	93	—	—	—	—		1.4	—	17.5	18.9	93
Total	173.8	56.9	1,389.0	1,619.7		253.6	19.7	256.7	530.0		513.1	76.6	1,645.7	2,149.7	100
Non-oak group—															
Bigleaf maple	—	—	—	—		2.9	—	—	2.9	100	2.9	—	—	2.9	100
Buckeye	6.3	—	—	6.3	100	—	—	—	—		6.3	—	—	6.3	100
California laurel	—	—	—	—		—	—	15.6	15.6	71	—	—	15.6	15.6	71
Dogwood	—	—	—	—		1.9	—	—	1.9	100	1.9	—	—	1.9	100
Pacific madrone	—	—	—	—		10.2	—	13.7	23.9	52	10.2	—	13.7	23.9	52
Tanoak	—	—	—	—		10.2	—	19.6	29.8	38	10.2	—	19.6	29.8	38
White alder	—	—	—	—		—	—	3.1	3.1	100	—	—	3.1	3.1	100
Willow	—	—	2.9	2.9	100	—	—	—	—		—	—	2.9	2.9	100
Total	6.3	—	2.9	9.2	100	25.2	—	51.9	77.1	100	31.5	—	54.8	86.3	
Total, Sacramento	180.1	56.9	1,391.9	1,628.9	4	278.8	19.7	308.6	607.1	9	544.6	76.6	1,700.5	2,236.0	
SE for total (%)	13	22	5		4	11	49	14		9	8	21	5		4

63

Table 2—Area of hardwood forest types on woodland and timberland by resource area and owner, California, 1990s (continued)

Resource area and forest type	Woodland					Timberland					Total				
	National forest	Other public	Private	Total Area	SE	National forest	Other public	Private	Total Area	SE	National forest	Other public	Private	Total Area	SE
	Thousand acres				%	*Thousand acres*				%	*Thousand acres*				%
Central Coast:															
Oak group—															
Blue oak[a]	66.7	91.1	429.7	587.4	13	—	—	3.9	3.9	100	66.7	91.1	433.6	591.3	13
Canyon live oak	63.6	—	—	63.6	27	36.5	—	12.8	49.3	35	100.1	—	12.8	112.9	21
Coast live oak	122.8	57.6	585.0	765.4	11	3.7	—	39.6	43.3	50	126.5	57.6	624.6	808.7	10
Interior live oak	7.3	—	13.7	21.0	71	4.4	—	—	4.4	72	11.7	—	13.7	25.4	60
Oregon white oak	—	—	5.9	5.9	77	—	—	—	—		—	—	5.9	5.9	77
Valley oak	—	—	53.7	53.7	50	—	—	—	—		—	—	53.7	53.7	50
Total	260.4	148.6	1,087.9	1,496.9		44.6	—	56.3	100.9		305.0	148.6	1,144.2	1,597.8	
Non-oak group—															
Bigleaf maple	17.9	—	3.5	21.4	50	—	—	—	—		17.9	—	3.5	21.4	50
California laurel	4.8	—	41.2	46.0	53	1.8	—	11.5	13.3	88	6.6	—	52.7	59.3	46
Eucalyptus	—	—	17.5	17.5	100	—	—	—	—		—	—	17.5	17.5	100
Pacific madrone	8.3	—	17.5	25.8	74	18.6	—	6.6	25.2	45	26.9	—	24.1	51.0	43
Sycamore	—	19.5	—	19.5	100	—	—	—	—		—	19.5	—	19.5	100
Tanoak	—	—	—	—		—	—	47.7	47.7	36	—	—	47.7	47.7	36
Willow	—	—	—	—		—	—	2.4	2.4	100	—	—	2.4	2.4	100
Other hardwoods	8.3	—	—	8.3	100	3.0	—	—	3.0	80	11.3	—	—	11.3	77
Total	39.3	19.5	79.6	138.4		23.4	—	68.2	91.6		62.7	19.5	147.8	230.0	
Total, Central Coast	299.7	168.1	1,167.6	1,635.4		68.0	—	124.4	192.4		367.7	168.1	1,292.0	1,827.8	
SE for total (%)	11	16	6	5		22	—	20	15		9	16	6	5	

Table 2—Area of hardwood forest types on woodland and timberland by resource area and owner, California, 1990s (continued)

Resource area and forest type	Woodland					Timberland					Total				
	National forest	Other public	Private	Total Area	SE	National forest	Other public	Private	Total Area	SE	National forest	Other public	Private	Total Area	SE
	Thousand acres				%	Thousand acres				%	Thousand acres				%
Southern:															
Oak group[a]—															
Blue oak	46.8	18.7	1,051.3	1,116.8	8	—	—	—	—	—	46.8	18.7	1,051.3	1,116.8	8
California black oak	50.3	2.5	18.7	71.5	32	198.5	6.7	41.8	247.0	14	248.8	9.2	60.5	318.6	13
Canyon live oak	251.5	19.5	59.3	330.3	15	119.8	11.5	68.4	199.7	15	371.3	30.9	127.7	529.9	11
Coast live oak	57.2	12.0	61.6	130.8	21	0.8	—	6.7	7.5	74	58.0	12.0	68.3	138.3	20
Engelmann oak	—	—	63.3	63.3	41	—	—	—	—	—	—	—	63.3	63.3	41
Interior live oak	88.7	97.7	531.9	718.2	12	20.6	—	20.9	41.5	35	109.3	97.7	552.8	759.7	11
Oregon white oak	—	—	12.9	12.9	100	—	—	—	—	—	—	—	12.9	12.9	100
Total	494.5	150.4	1,799.0	2,443.8		339.7	18.2	137.8	495.7		834.2	168.5	1,936.8	2,939.5	
Non-oak group—															
Bigleaf maple	2.4	—	—	2.4	100	—	—	—	—	—	2.4	—	—	2.4	100
Buckeye	28.8	—	74.0	102.8	35	6.2	—	—	6.2	100	35.0	—	74.0	109.0	34
California laurel	17.0	—	—	17.0	54	—	—	—	—	—	17.0	—	—	17.0	54
Cottonwood/aspen	24.6	—	—	24.6	55	5.3	12.7	—	18.0	75	29.9	12.7	—	42.6	45
Eucalyptus	—	—	8.5	8.5	100	—	—	—	—	—	—	—	8.5	8.5	100
Oregon ash	4.0	—	—	4.0	100	—	—	—	—	—	4.0	—	—	4.0	100
Sycamore	1.5	—	—	1.5	100	—	—	—	—	—	1.5	—	—	1.5	100
Walnut	—	—	5.7	5.8	100	—	—	—	—	—	—	—	5.7	5.8	100
White alder	8.2	—	16.1	24.3	71	5.6	—	3.5	9.1	51	13.8	—	19.6	33.4	54
Willow	—	—	11.4	11.4	100	—	—	—	—	—	—	—	11.4	11.4	100
Other hardwoods	18.6	—	—	18.6	52	0.4	—	—	0.4	100	19.0	—	—	19.0	50
Total	105.1	—	115.8	220.9		17.5	12.7	3.5	33.7		122.6	12.7	119.3	254.6	
Total, Southern	599.6	150.4	1,914.8	2,664.8	3	357.2	30.9	141.3	529.4	9	956.8	181.3	2,056.1	3,194.2	3
SE for total (%)	7	18	4	3		11	48	20	9		5	17	4	3	

65

Table 2—Area of hardwood forest types on woodland and timberland by resource area and owner, California, 1990s (continued)

Resource area and forest type	Woodland National forest	Other public	Private	Total Area	SE %	Timberland National forest	Other public	Private	Total Area	SE %	Total National forest	Other public	Private	Total Area	SE %
	— — — Thousand acres — — —					— — — Thousand acres — — —					— — — Thousand acres — — —				
Total, California:															
Oak group—															
Blue oak[a]	130.7	170.2	2,723.6	3,024.5	5	—	—	3.9	3.9	100	216.4	170.2	2,727.5	3,028.4	5
California black oak	123.2	2.5	161.6	287.3	17	481.0	16.5	470.0	967.5	8	604.2	19.0	631.6	1,254.8	7
Canyon live oak	574.8	49.8	198.8	823.4	9	422.3	64.6	314.7	801.6	9	997.1	114.4	513.5	1,625.0	6
Coast live oak	180.0	81.5	731.8	993.3	9	4.5	—	70.1	74.6	33	184.5	81.5	801.9	1,067.9	9
Engelmann oak	—	—	63.3	63.3	41	—	—	—	—	—	—	—	63.3	63.3	41
Interior live oak	114.8	97.7	818.2	1,030.6	10	40.7	1.9	66.9	109.5	22	155.5	99.6	885.1	1,140.1	9
Oregon white oak	86.4	28.3	265.4	380.1	15	29.6	9.2	161.2	200.1	17	116.0	37.5	426.6	580.1	12
Valley oak	1.4	—	129.0	130.4	33	8.0	—	13.2	21.2	54	9.4	—	142.2	151.6	29
Total	1,211.3	430.0	5,091.6	6,732.8		986.1	92.2	1,100.1	2,178.4		2,283.1	522.2	6,191.6	8,911.2	
Non-oak group—															
Bigleaf maple	26.0	—	12.6	38.6	41	15.3	3.4	31.6	50.3	37	41.3	3.4	44.1	88.9	28
Buckeye	35.1	—	78.3	113.4	32	6.2	—	—	6.2	100	41.3	—	78.3	119.6	31
California laurel	21.8	—	68.2	90.0	36	3.8	—	111.3	115.1	24	25.6	—	179.5	205.1	21
Cottonwood/aspen	24.6	—	7.2	31.9	48	25.9	14.4	5.2	45.5	39	50.5	14.4	12.4	77.3	31
Dogwood	—	—	—	—	—	1.9	—	3.2	5.1	73	1.9	—	3.2	5.1	73
Eucalyptus	—	—	25.9	25.9	79	—	—	3.6	3.6	100	—	—	29.5	29.5	69
Giant chinquapin	—	—	—	—	—	18.2	—	6.2	24.4	56	18.2	—	6.2	24.4	56
Oregon ash	4.0	—	16.5	20.5	85	—	—	—	—	—	4.0	—	16.5	20.5	85
Pacific madrone	17.6	—	47.0	64.6	46	104.5	11.4	167.7	283.6	15	122.1	11.4	214.6	348.1	15
Red alder	4.1	—	—	4.1	100	12.5	—	75.8	88.3	28	16.6	—	75.8	92.4	27
Sycamore	1.5	19.5	—	21.0	91	—	—	—	—	—	1.5	19.5	—	21.0	91
Tanoak	2.6	—	—	2.6	100	228.4	—	1,017.9	1,246.3	6	231.0	—	1,017.9	1,248.9	6
Walnut	—	—	5.7	5.8	100	—	—	—	—	—	0.0	—	5.7	5.8	100
White alder	8.2	—	16.1	24.3	71	5.6	—	6.6	12.2	46	13.8	—	22.7	36.5	51
Willow	—	—	14.4	14.4	84	—	—	12.0	12.0	60	—	—	26.4	26.4	54
Other hardwoods	26.9	—	—	26.9	47	3.4	—	—	3.4	71	30.3	—	—	30.3	43
Total	172.5	19.5	292.0	483.9		425.7	29.2	1,441.0	1,895.9		598.2	48.7	1,732.9	2,379.8	
Total, California	1,383.8	449.5	5,383.5	7,216.7		1,411.8	121.4	2,541.1	4,074.3		2,881.3	570.9	7,924.6	11,291.0	
SE for total (%)	5	10	2			5	24	4	3		3	9	2	2	

Note: Excludes reserved lands outside of national forests because these areas were not sampled.

SE = sampling error.

— = less than 50 acres.

[a] The blue oak forest type includes 110,000 acres initially classified as ghost pine (*Pinus sabiniana*).

Table 3—Net growing-stock volume of hardwood species on woodland and timberland by resource area and owner, California, 1990s

Resource area and species	Woodland					Timberland					Total				
	National forest	Other public	Private	Total Volume	SE %	National forest	Other public	Private	Total Volume	SE %	National forest	Other public	Private	Total Volume	SE %
	Million cubic feet					*Million cubic feet*					*Million cubic feet*				
North Coast:															
Oak group—															
Blue oak	—	—	32.3	32.3	53								32.3	32.3	53
California black oak	16.9	—	81.8	98.7	22	35.4	22.7	257.7	315.8	15	52.3	22.7	339.6	414.5	12
Canyon live oak	49.5	—	47.2	96.7	37	82.4	37.5	188.9	308.7	17	131.9	37.5	236.1	405.5	16
Coast live oak	—	4.8	55.1	59.8	36	—	—	22.6	22.6	37		4.8	77.7	82.5	29
Interior live oak	—	—	5.3	5.3	71	3.0	2.3	25.5	30.7	39	3.0	2.3	30.8	36.0	34
Oregon white oak	46.8	.7	164.0	211.5	26	3.0	6.2	178.1	187.3	19	49.8	6.9	342.1	398.8	17
Valley oak	—	—	28.8	28.8	55	—	—	25.5	25.5	44			54.4	54.4	37
Total	113.3	5.4	414.5	533.2		123.7	68.6	698.4	890.7		236.9	74.1	1,112.9	1,423.9	
Non-oak group—															
Bigleaf maple	3.6	—	6.0	9.6	51	26.6	4.8	69.9	101.2	22	30.2	4.8	75.8	110.8	20
Black cottonwood	—	—	—	—		—	—	6.8	6.8	94			6.8	6.8	94
California buckeye	—	—	1.3	1.3	75								1.3	1.3	75
California laurel	—	—	58.9	58.9	50	6.6	6.4	194.4	207.3	15	6.6	6.4	253.3	266.3	17
Eucalyptus	—	—	—	—				15.3	15.3	80			15.3	15.3	80
Giant chinquapin	—	—	—	—		29.6		20.8	50.5	35	29.6		20.8	50.5	35
Oregon ash	—	—	—	—				1.3	1.3	99			1.3	1.3	99
Pacific madrone	9.6	1.7	69.2	80.6	35	154.2	52.5	688.7	895.5	9	163.9	54.3	758.0	976.1	9
Red alder	—	—	—	—		2.5		203.6	206.1	23	2.5		203.6	206.1	23
Tanoak	—	—	—	—		278.6	35.7	1,499.0	1,813.3	7	278.6	35.7	1,499.0	1,813.3	7
White alder	—	—	—	—		1.0		—	1.0	74	1.0		—	1.0	74
Total	13.2	1.7	135.4	150.3		499.2	99.3	2,699.9	3,298.4		512.5	101.1	2,835.3	3,448.8	
Total, North Coast	126.5	7.2	549.9	683.6	11	622.9	168.0	3,398.2	4,189.1	5	749.4	175.1	3,948.1	4,872.7	5
SE for total (%)	35	87	12	11		19	22	5	5		17	21	5	5	

Table 3—Net growing-stock volume of hardwood species on woodland and timberland by resource area and owner, California, 1990s (continued)

Resource area and species	Woodland					Timberland					Total				
	National forest	Other public	Private	Total Volume	SE	National forest	Other public	Private	Total Volume	SE	National forest	Other public	Private	Total Volume	SE
	Million cubic feet				%	*Million cubic feet*				%	*Million cubic feet*				%
North Interior:															
Oak group—															
Blue oak	—	1.5	86.4	87.9	27	—	—	—	—		—	1.5	86.4	87.9	27
California black oak	53.8	4.1	38.1	96.0	26	355.6	30.3	358.1	744.0	8	409.4	34.4	396.2	840.0	8
Canyon live oak	112.0	12.6	17.4	142.0	25	452.7	26.2	188.2	667.1	11	564.7	38.9	205.6	809.2	10
Coast live oak						.2	—	—	.2	100	.2	—	—	.2	100
Interior live oak	12.0	—	13.1	25.1	47	21.7	—	.5	22.1	33	33.7	—	13.6	47.2	29
Oregon white oak	27.5	12.6	43.4	83.5	30	31.5	7.2	37.6	76.4	20	59.0	19.8	81.1	159.9	18
Valley oak	.7	—	18.9	19.6	60	2.1	—	.7	2.8	39	2.8	—	19.6	22.4	53
Total	206.0	30.8	217.3	454.1		863.8	63.8	585.1	1,512.7		1,069.8	94.7	802.4	1,966.8	
Non-oak group—															
Bigleaf maple	21.7	—	1.7	23.4	57	62.4	3.1	34.9	100.4	21	84.0	3.1	36.6	123.8	20
Black cottonwood	—	—	9.0	9.0	100	.1	1.3	—	1.4	95	.1	1.3	9.0	10.4	88
California laurel						1.8	—	8.0	9.8	68	1.8	—	8.0	9.8	68
Eucalyptus						—	—	—	—	100	—	—	—	.2	100
Giant chinquapin	1.3	—	—	1.3	100	21.6	—	4.5	26.1	32	22.9	—	4.5	27.4	31
Oregon ash						.8	—	—	.8	100	.8	—	—	0.8	100
Pacific madrone	21.6	—	2.1	23.6	74	305.6	—	39.6	345.3	13	327.2	—	41.7	368.9	13
Quaking aspen						26.1	—	11.3	37.4	55	26.1	—	11.3	37.4	55
Red alder	.4	—	—	.4	100	13.5	—	—	13.5	39	13.9	—	—	13.9	38
Tanoak	3.1	—	—	3.1	100	132.8	—	27.3	160.2	24	136.0	—	27.3	163.3	24
White alder	.7	—	—	.7	100	6.3	—	8.6	14.9	46	6.9	—	8.6	15.5	45
Total	48.7	—	12.8	61.6		571.0	4.4	134.3	709.7		619.8	4.4	147.1	771.3	
Total, North Interior	254.7	30.8	230.1	515.7	14	1,434.8	68.3	719.3	2,222.4	6	1,689.5	99.1	949.5	2,738.1	5
SE for total (%)	22	49	18	14		7	33	9	6		7	27	8	5	

Table 3—Net growing-stock volume of hardwood species on woodland and timberland by resource area and owner, California, 1990s (continued)

Resource area and species	Woodland					Timberland					Total				
	National forest	Other public	Private	Total Volume	Total SE %	National forest	Other public	Private	Total Volume	Total SE %	National forest	Other public	Private	Total Volume	Total SE %
	— — — — Million cubic feet — — — —					*— — — — Million cubic feet — — — —*					*— — — — Million cubic feet — — — —*				
Sacramento:															
Oak group—															
Blue oak	—	10.0	432.3	442.3	12	—	—	2.6	2.6	100	—	10.0	434.9	444.8	12
California black oak	58.4	—	78.6	137.0	21	450.7	14.4	513.6	978.7	8	509.1	14.4	592.2	1,115.8	8
Canyon live oak	124.0	10.5	51.8	186.3	22	223.8	32.6	135.1	391.5	14	347.8	43.0	186.9	577.8	12
Interior live oak	—	3.6	75.9	79.5	25	4.5	.1	16.3	20.9	36	4.5	3.7	92.2	100.4	21
Oregon white oak	.2	—	—	.2	100	.9	—	.5	1.4	75	1.2	—	.5	1.6	66
Valley oak	2.5	—	33.0	35.5	78	—	—	—	—		2.5	—	33.0	35.5	78
Total	185.2	24.1	671.6	880.8		679.9	47.1	668.1	1,395.1		865.1	71.1	1,339.7	2,275.9	
Non-oak group—															
Bigleaf maple	6.0	—	8.7	14.6	54	8.8	—	29.1	37.9	25	14.8	—	37.7	52.6	24
Black cottonwood	—	—	—	—		—	—	5.0	5.0	83	—	—	5.0	5.0	83
California laurel	.2	—	—	.2	100	3.6	—	10.1	13.7	53	3.8	—	10.1	14.0	52
California sycamore	.2	—	—	.2	100	—	—	—	—		.2	—	—	.2	100
Oregon ash	.2	—	—	.2	100	—	—	—	—		.2	—	—	.2	100
Pacific madrone	.3	—	—	.3	72	42.7	2.0	55.1	99.9	20	43.0	2.0	55.1	100.2	20
Quaking aspen	.2	—	—	.2	100	1.7	—	2.3	4.0	64	1.9	—	2.3	4.2	62
Red alder	—	—	—	—		2.5	—	10.4	12.9	53	2.5	—	10.4	12.9	53
Tanoak	—	—	—	—		41.6	—	50.5	92.1	21	41.6	—	50.5	92.1	21
White alder	.9	—	—	.9	100	1.7	—	10.3	12.1	47	2.7	—	10.3	13.0	44
Total	8.0	—	8.7	16.6		102.7	2.0	172.8	277.6		110.7	2.0	181.5	294.2	
Total, Sacramento	193.1	24.1	680.3	897.4	9	782.6	49.1	840.9	1,672.7	6	975.8	73.2	1,521.2	2,570.1	5
SE for total (%)	15	42	12	9		8	26	10	6		7	22	8	5	

Table 3—Net growing-stock volume of hardwood species on woodland and timberland by resource area and owner, California, 1990s (continued)

Resource area and species	Woodland					Timberland					Total				
	National forest	Other public	Private	Total Volume	SE %	National forest	Other public	Private	Total Volume	SE %	National forest	Other public	Private	Total Volume	SE %
	Million cubic feet					*Million cubic feet*					*Million cubic feet*				
Central Coast:															
Oak group—															
Blue oak	—	20.8	160.3	181.1	17	—	—	1.2	1.2	100	—	20.8	161.5	182.3	17
California black oak	—	—	15.2	15.2	63	6.9	—	2.0	8.8	59	6.9	—	17.2	24.1	45
Canyon live oak	2.3	—	6.9	9.2	75	18.3	—	47.3	65.6	74	20.7	—	54.2	74.8	66
Coast live oak	54.2	35.8	583.9	673.9	14	1.4	—	109.6	111.0	43	55.6	35.8	693.6	784.9	14
Interior live oak	—	—	33.6	33.6	100	2.4	—	—	2.4	94	2.4	—	33.6	36.0	93
Oregon white oak	—	—	13.4	13.4	80	—	—	—	—		—	—	14.9	14.9	72
Valley oak	—	—	90.7	90.7	36	—	—	1.5	1.5	101	—	—	90.7	90.7	36
Total	56.5	56.5	904.0	1,017.1		29.0	—	161.6	190.5		85.5	56.5	1,065.6	1,207.6	
Non-oak group—															
Bigleaf maple	1.3	—	20.6	21.9	77	—	—	.9	.9	72	1.3	—	21.5	22.8	74
California buckeye	—	—	2.2	2.2	100	—	—	—	—	100	—	—	2.2	2.2	100
California laurel	.4	3.8	80.6	84.8	38	.8	—	48.6	49.4	59	1.2	3.8	129.2	134.2	33
California sycamore	3.4	11.2	31.7	46.3	41	—	—	—	—		3.4	11.2	31.7	46.3	41
Eucalyptus	—	—	96.0	96.0	100	—	—	4.3	4.3	100	—	—	100.3	100.3	95
Pacific madrone	2.0	25.5	22.7	50.2	63	4.9	—	77.1	82.0	32	6.9	25.5	99.8	132.2	30
Tanoak	—	—	—	—		2.1	—	163.7	165.8	39	2.1	—	163.7	165.8	39
Other hardwoods	—	—	—	—		11.3	—	—	11.3	73	11.3	—	—	11.3	73
Total	7.2	40.5	253.8	301.5		19.1	—	294.5	313.7		26.3	40.5	548.4	615.1	
Total, Central Coast	63.7	97.0	1,157.9	1,318.6		48.1	—	456.1	504.2	18	111.8	97.0	1,614.0	1,822.8	10
SE for total (%)	39	43	13	12		30		20	18		25	43	11	10	

Table 3—Net growing-stock volume of hardwood species on woodland and timberland by resource area and owner, California, 1990s (continued)

Resource area and species	Woodland					Timberland					Total				
	National forest	Other public	Private	Total Volume	SE	National forest	Other public	Private	Total Volume	SE	National forest	Other public	Private	Total Volume	SE
	Million cubic feet				%	Million cubic feet				%	Million cubic feet				%
Southern:															
Oak group—															
Blue oak	—	17.4	409.0	426.4	13	—	—	—	—	—	—	17.4	409.0	426.4	13
California black oak	67.2	9.1	8.6	84.9	29	290.4	10.3	203.7	504.5	10	357.6	19.4	212.3	589.4	9
Canyon live oak	162.9	19.4	84.8	267.0	20	122.3	20.2	95.8	238.3	16	285.2	39.6	180.6	505.3	13
Coast live oak	47.5	16.4	45.2	109.2	16	.8	—	1.5	2.3	68	48.3	16.4	46.8	111.5	16
Engelmann oak	—	—	38.6	38.6	58	—	—	—	—	—	—	—	38.6	38.6	58
Interior live oak	31.1	12.0	197.2	240.3	18	3.7	—	2.0	5.7	51	34.9	12.0	199.2	246.0	17
Oregon white oak	—	—	1.1	1.1	100	—	—	.2	.2	100	—	—	1.4	1.4	85
Valley oak	—	—	19.4	19.4	55	—	—	7.7	7.7	54	—	—	27.1	27.1	43
Total	308.7	74.3	804.0	1,187.0		417.3	30.6	310.9	758.8		726.0	104.8	1,114.9	1,945.7	
Non-oak group—															
Bigleaf maple	6.5	—	—	6.5	64	6.4	—	2.1	8.5	41	12.9	—	2.1	15.0	36
Black cottonwood	.2	—	—	.2	75	—	—	—	—	—	.2	—	—	.2	75
California buckeye	—	1.3	12.2	13.4	46	—	—	—	—	—	—	1.3	12.2	13.4	46
California laurel	3.8	—	—	3.8	54	—	.3	1.1	1.4	81	3.8	.3	1.1	5.3	45
California sycamore	.8	—	—	.8	55	—	—	—	—	—	.8	—	—	.8	55
Eucalyptus	—	—	10.1	10.1	100	—	—	—	—	—	—	—	10.1	10.1	100
Oregon ash	4.9	—	—	4.9	98	.8	1.5	—	2.3	75	5.7	1.5	—	7.2	71
Pacific madrone	—	—	—	—	—	—	—	2.3	2.3	101	—	—	2.3	2.3	101
Quaking aspen	2.2	—	—	2.2	100	2.6	—	2.7	5.3	63	4.8	—	2.7	7.5	53
Red alder	—	—	—	—	—	.8	—	—	.8	100	.8	—	—	.8	100
Tanoak	—	—	—	—	—	—	—	.7	.7	79	—	—	.7	.7	79
Walnut	—	—	—	—	—	—	—	1.1	1.1	100	—	—	1.1	1.1	100
White alder	6.8	—	2.4	9.2	44	13.0	—	11.7	24.7	33	19.8	—	14.1	33.9	27
Total	25.3	1.3	24.7	51.2		23.6	1.8	21.7	47.1		48.9	3.1	46.4	98.3	
Total, Southern	334.0	75.5	828.7	1,238.2	7	440.9	32.4	332.6	805.9	9	774.9	107.9	1,161.3	2,044.1	5
SE for total (%)	10	36	9	7		9	33	17	9		6	28	8	5	

Table 3—Net growing-stock volume of hardwood species on woodland and timberland by resource area and owner, California, 1990s (continued)

Resource area and species	Woodland National forest	Woodland Other public	Woodland Private	Woodland Total Volume	Woodland SE %	Timberland National forest	Timberland Other public	Timberland Private	Timberland Total Volume	Timberland SE %	Total National forest	Total Other public	Total Private	Total Total Volume	Total SE %
	— — — — Million cubic feet — — — —					*— — — — Million cubic feet — — — —*					*— — — — Million cubic feet — — — —*				
Total, California:															
Oak group—															
Blue oak	—	49.6	1,120.2	1,169.9	8	—	—	3.8	3.8	75	—	49.6	1,124.0	1,173.7	8
California black oak	196.4	13.2	222.4	431.9	12	1,139.0	77.7	1,335.2	2,551.9	5	1,335.3	90.9	1,557.5	2,983.8	4
Canyon live oak	450.8	42.5	208.1	701.3	12	899.5	116.5	655.3	1,671.3	7	1,350.2	159.0	863.4	2,372.6	6
Coast live oak	101.7	57.0	684.3	842.9	12	2.4	—	133.8	136.2	36	104.1	57.0	818.0	979.1	11
Engelmann oak	—	—	38.6	38.6	58	—	—	—	—	—	—	—	38.6	38.6	58
Interior live oak	43.2	15.6	325.0	383.8	15	35.2	2.4	44.2	81.9	20	78.4	18.0	369.3	465.6	13
Oregon white oak	74.5	13.3	222.0	309.8	20	35.4	13.4	218.0	266.8	15	110.0	26.7	439.9	576.6	13
Valley oak	3.2	—	190.8	194.0	25	2.1	—	33.9	36.0	34	5.2	—	224.7	230.0	21
Total	869.6	191.1	3,011.4	4,072.2		2,113.6	210.1	2,424.1	4,747.8		2,983.3	401.2	5,435.5	8,820.0	
Non-oak group—															
Bigleaf maple	39.0	—	36.9	75.9	30	104.2	7.9	136.8	248.9	13	143.2	7.9	173.8	324.9	12
Black cottonwood	.2	—	9.0	9.2	98	.1	1.3	11.8	13.2	60	.3	1.3	20.8	22.4	54
California buckeye	—	1.3	15.6	16.9	39	—	—	—	—	—	—	1.3	15.6	16.9	39
California laurel	4.5	3.8	139.6	147.9	30	12.8	6.7	262.2	281.7	16	17.3	10.5	401.7	429.5	15
California sycamore	4.4	11.2	31.7	47.3	40	—	—	—	—	—	4.4	11.2	31.7	47.3	40
Eucalyptus	—	—	106.1	106.1	93	—	—	19.6	19.6	66	—	—	125.7	125.7	78
Giant chinquapin	1.3	—	—	1.3	100	51.2	—	25.3	76.5	25	52.5	—	25.3	77.8	25
Oregon ash	5.1	—	—	5.1	94	1.6	1.5	1.3	4.4	52	6.7	1.5	1.3	9.5	56
Pacific madrone	33.5	27.2	94.0	154.8	29	507.5	54.6	862.9	1,425.0	7	541.0	81.8	956.9	1,579.7	7
Quaking aspen	2.4	—	—	2.4	93	30.4	—	16.3	46.8	45	32.8	—	16.3	49.2	43
Red alder	.4	—	—	.4	100	19.4	—	214.0	233.3	21	19.8	—	214.0	233.7	21
Tanoak	3.1	—	—	3.1	100	455.2	35.7	1,741.2	2,232.0	7	458.3	35.7	1,741.2	2,235.2	7
Walnut	—	—	—	—	—	—	—	1.1	1.1	100	—	—	1.1	1.1	100
White alder	8.4	—	2.4	10.8	39	22.1	—	30.6	52.7	23	30.4	—	33.0	63.4	20
Other hardwoods	—	—	—	—		11.3	—	—	11.3	69	11.3	—	—	11.3	69
Total	102.4	43.5	435.4	581.2	5	1,215.7	107.6	3,323.2	4,646.6	3	1,318.1	151.1	3,758.6	5,227.8	3
Total, California	972.0	234.6	3,446.8	4,653.4	5	3,329.4	317.7	5,747.3	9,394.3	3	4,301.4	552.3	9,194.0	14,047.7	3
SE for total (%)	9	22	6	5		5	15	4	3		4	12	3	3	

Note: Excludes reserved lands outside of national forests because these areas were not sampled.

Excludes cull trees and cull volume; includes growing-stock trees ≥5 inches diameter at breast height.

SE= sampling error.

— = less than 50,000 cubic feet.

72

Table 4—Total stem volume of hardwood species for all live trees on woodland by diameter class, California, 1990s

Species	Diameter class (inches at breast height)											All classes	
	1.0-4.9	5.0-8.9	9.0-12.9	13.0-16.9	17.0-20.9	21.0-24.9	25.0-28.9	29.0-32.9	33.0-36.9	37.0-40.9	41.0+	Total	SE
	Million cubic feet												%
Oak group:													
Blue oak	104.9	522.3	761.6	463.0	375.2	248.0	149.5	74.9	11.4	19.0	—	2,729.6	6
California black oak	26.6	134.5	155.5	148.4	96.1	78.7	53.5	20.2	22.6	15.7	11.9	763.7	11
Canyon live oak	108.5	403.9	356.3	214.0	121.7	77.8	52.5	48.1	25.8	13.5	69.1	1,491.1	10
Coast live oak	17.3	149.7	332.3	507.7	420.8	225.0	155.9	113.7	92.8	34.1	26.2	2,075.6	11
Engelmann oak	5.8	10.1	7.2	15.6	3.5	28.4	10.6	14.1	—	—	—	95.3	50
Interior live oak	223.2	407.6	241.3	126.1	88.0	32.9	11.5	23.5	3.3	2.4	12.8	1,172.6	12
Oregon white oak	35.7	163.8	128.0	78.7	70.8	32.3	17.5	22.3	12.0	11.4	10.1	582.5	17
Valley oak	.6	4.9	64.3	34.8	39.4	25.6	46.6	46.6	43.8	11.6	43.2	361.4	21
Total	522.4	1,796.8	2,046.5	1,588.4	1,215.5	748.7	497.6	363.4	211.6	107.7	173.2	9,271.8	4
Non-oak group:													
Bigleaf maple	6.1	42.3	32.9	25.5	22.1	9.7	4.8	6.7	4.1	6.8	10.2	171.1	26
Black cottonwood	—	—	.1		.2						9.8	10.1	98
California buckeye	13.9	63.3	29.3	19.1		.2					—	125.8	20
California laurel	27.3	71.9	63.2	48.0	23.7	15.7	20.5	5.3			—	270.5	27
California sycamore	1.8	7.1	1.0	16.0	3.5	21.2	14.1		5.5		—	75.7	42
Eucalyptus	1.1	19.8	32.8	17.7	25.0	15.6				5.8	—	117.8	94
Giant chinquapin				1.8							—	1.8	100
Oregon ash	.4	4.1	1.0	2.6	1.5	.6	.7				—	11.0	71
Pacific madrone	12.6	38.4	104.6	36.4	18.1	14.4	13.4	3.8			—	241.8	26
Quaking aspen	3.1	3.6			1.3			.7			—	8.7	78
Red alder		.4									—	.5	95
Tanoak	1.8	3.1	2.7	1.6	5.9	4.3	4.2	.7	.5		—	24.8	64
White alder	1.1	1.3	5.8	2.8	1.5	1.3	.2	2.4			3.0	19.4	42
Willow	3.2	10.4	16.3	6.3	7.0	11.1	6.8				—	61.1	58
Other hardwoods[a]	2.5	10.5	6.3	7.5	4.1	1.9	1.2			2.4	—	36.5	41
Total	74.9	276.4	295.9	185.3	114.0	96.1	66.1	19.7	10.1	15.0	23.0	1,176.5	14
Total, California	597.4	2,073.1	2,342.5	1,773.8	1,329.4	844.8	563.7	383.0	221.7	122.7	196.2	10,448.3	4
SE for total (%)	8	6	5	6	6	8	9	11	17	23	21	4	

Note: Excludes reserved lands outside of national forests because these areas were not sampled.

Includes sound and rotten cull trees.

SE = sampling error.

— = less than 50,000 cubic feet.

[a] Other hardwoods includes apple, walnut, and unknowns.

Table 5—Total stem volume of hardwood species for all live trees on timberland by diameter class, California, 1990s

| Species | Diameter class (inches at breast height) Million cubic feet | | | | | | | | | | | All classes | |
	1.0-4.9	5.0-8.9	9.0-12.9	13.0-16.9	17.0-20.9	21.0-24.9	25.0-28.9	29.0-32.9	33.0-36.9	37.0-40.9	41.0+	Total	SE %
Oak group:													
Blue oak	0.2	1.7	—	2.4	4.8	1.6	—	—	—	—	3.9	14.6	51
California black oak	148.0	687.8	856.7	717.5	534.8	474.1	315.9	262.6	143.1	91.5	141.9	4,373.7	4
Canyon live oak	176.2	660.2	678.4	453.0	327.6	237.4	149.1	116.7	78.5	52.0	59.3	2,988.4	6
Coast live oak	2.6	25.3	53.7	61.9	69.8	32.7	25.3	6.8	2.7	8.9	—	289.7	33
Interior live oak	25.7	39.8	26.9	24.4	20.6	17.3	6.4	4.4	4.7	7.2	2.4	179.7	18
Oregon white oak	37.5	181.3	124.9	60.8	52.1	38.7	10.1	10.5	3.5	10.9	7.7	538.0	13
Valley oak	2.9	11.4	11.6	6.2	4.9	7.3	8.7	5.4	—	—	—	58.4	32
Total	392.9	1,607.6	1,752.2	1,326.1	1,014.6	809.0	515.4	406.3	232.5	170.5	215.3	8,442.4	4
Non-oak group:													
Bigleaf maple	32.7	98.8	97.5	68.7	51.6	33.0	6.5	15.2	1.7	9.2	5.6	420.6	12
Black cottonwood	.3	2.2	1.0	.1	.2	5.2	1.4	—	4.5	—	—	14.9	56
California buckeye	1.3	3.9	2.4	—	—	1.8	—	—	—	—	—	9.4	38
California laurel	44.7	117.0	110.9	96.6	43.5	30.5	12.4	9.9	7.6	—	3.4	476.5	14
Eucalyptus	—	—	—	—	—	5.7	2.9	2.6	—	—	9.9	21.1	67
Giant chinquapin	9.0	25.2	30.2	24.1	14.8	6.8	11.1	4.2	—	—	—	125.4	22
Oregon ash	1.3	.4	1.9	2.9	—	—	—	—	1.0	—	—	7.6	53
Pacific dogwood	17.4	3.4	4.6	—	.8	—	—	—	—	—	—	26.2	17
Pacific madrone	65.6	284.0	368.9	430.4	331.6	235.0	162.0	84.7	58.9	45.6	76.5	2,143.1	6
Quaking aspen	2.2	6.4	15.7	20.5	4.3	11.5	.2	—	.5	—	—	61.3	38
Red alder	20.5	80.3	111.3	46.8	18.8	11.5	8.6	3.7	2.5	—	4.2	308.2	19
Tanoak	429.4	1,059.1	1,074.4	744.2	563.3	335.4	201.0	123.2	38.2	11.2	38.2	4,617.6	6
White alder	3.4	10.3	13.8	16.6	13.0	5.2	3.6	.2	1.5	1.6	—	69.3	22
Willow	4.7	6.4	7.5	3.6	1.0	—	—	—	—	—	—	23.2	33
Other hardwoods [a]	3.6	4.8	4.7	3.8	4.0	6.6	6.4	.5	.8	.3	2.2	37.9	35
Total	636.2	1,702.2	1,844.8	1,458.4	1,047.1	688.2	416.0	244.1	117.2	68.0	140.0	8,362.3	4
Total, California	1,029.0	3,309.8	3,597.0	2,784.6	2,061.7	1,497.2	931.4	650.4	349.7	238.4	355.3	16,804.7	
SE for total (%)	4	4	4	4	5	5	6	7	9	12	13	3	

Note: Excludes reserved lands outside of national forests because these areas were not sampled.

Includes sound and rotten cull trees.

SE = sampling error.

— = less than 50,000 cubic feet.

[a] Other hardwoods includes apple, walnut, and unknowns.

Table 6—Total stem volume of hardwood species for all live trees on woodland and timberland by diameter class, California, 1990s

Species	Diameter class (inches at breast height)											All classes	
	1.0- 4.9	5.0- 8.9	9.0- 12.9	13.0- 16.9	17.0- 20.9	21.0- 24.9	25.0- 28.9	29.0- 32.9	33.0- 36.9	37.0- 40.9	41.0 +	Total	SE %
	------ Million cubic feet ------												
Oak group:													
Blue oak	105.0	524.0	761.6	465.4	380.0	249.5	149.5	74.9	11.4	19.0	3.9	2,744.2	6
California black oak	174.5	822.3	1,012.2	865.9	630.9	552.8	369.3	282.8	165.7	107.2	153.8	5,137.4	4
Canyon live oak	284.7	1,064.1	1,034.7	667.0	449.3	315.1	201.6	164.8	104.3	65.4	128.4	4,479.5	5
Coast live oak	19.8	175.1	386.1	569.6	490.6	257.7	181.2	120.5	95.5	43.1	26.2	2,365.3	11
Engelmann oak	5.8	10.1	7.2	15.6	3.5	28.4	10.6	14.1	—	—	—	95.3	50
Interior live oak	248.8	447.4	268.2	150.5	108.6	50.1	17.9	27.9	8.0	9.6	15.2	1,352.3	11
Oregon white oak	73.1	345.1	252.9	139.5	123.0	71.1	27.6	32.8	15.5	22.3	17.8	1,120.5	11
Valley oak	3.4	16.3	75.9	41.0	44.3	32.9	55.3	52.0	43.8	11.6	43.2	419.8	19
Total	915.3	3,404.3	3,798.8	2,914.5	2,230.1	1,557.7	1,013.0	769.7	444.1	278.2	388.5	17,714.2	3
Non-oak group:													
Bigleaf maple	38.8	141.1	130.3	94.2	73.7	42.8	11.3	22.0	5.8	16.0	15.8	591.7	11
Black cottonwood	.3	2.2	1.1	.1	.4	5.2	1.4	—	4.5	—	9.8	25.0	52
California buckeye	15.2	67.2	31.7	19.1	—	2.0	—	—	—	—	—	135.2	19
California laurel	72.0	188.9	174.1	144.7	67.2	46.2	33.0	9.9	7.6	—	3.4	747.0	13
California sycamore	1.8	7.1	1.0	16.0	3.5	21.2	14.1	5.3	5.5	—	—	75.7	42
Eucalyptus	1.1	19.9	32.8	17.7	25.0	21.2	2.9	2.6	—	5.8	9.9	138.9	79
Giant chinquapin	9.0	25.2	30.2	25.9	14.8	6.8	11.1	4.2	—	—	—	127.2	22
Oregon ash	1.8	4.5	2.9	5.5	1.5	.6	.7	—	1.0	—	—	18.6	47
Pacific dogwood	17.4	3.4	4.6	—	.8	—	—	—	—	—	—	26.2	17
Pacific madrone	78.2	322.4	473.5	466.9	349.7	249.3	175.4	88.5	58.9	45.6	76.5	2,384.9	6
Quaking aspen	5.2	10.0	15.7	20.5	5.6	11.5	.2	.7	.5	—	—	70.0	34
Red alder	20.5	80.7	111.3	46.8	18.8	11.5	8.6	3.7	2.5	—	4.2	308.7	19
Tanoak	431.2	1,062.2	1,077.0	745.8	569.2	339.8	205.2	124.0	38.7	11.2	38.2	4,642.4	6
White alder	4.6	11.5	19.6	19.5	14.5	6.5	3.8	2.6	1.5	1.6	3.0	88.8	20
Willow	7.9	16.8	23.8	9.9	8.0	11.1	6.8	—	—	—	—	84.4	43
Other hardwoods [a]	6.1	15.4	11.2	11.4	8.1	8.6	7.6	.5	.8	2.7	2.2	74.6	27
Total	711.1	1,978.6	2,140.9	1,643.8	1,161.1	784.3	482.1	263.8	127.4	83.0	163.0	9,539.0	4
Total, California	1,626.4	5,383.0	5,939.7	4,558.4	3,391.2	2,342.0	1,495.1	1,033.4	571.5	361.2	551.4	27,253.2	2
SE for total (%)	4	3	3	3	4	4	5	6	9	11	11	2	

Note: Excludes reserved lands outside of national forests because these areas were not sampled.

Includes sound and rotten cull trees.

SE = sampling error.

— = less than 50,000 cubic feet.

[a] Other hardwoods includes apple, walnut, and unknowns.

Table 7—Aboveground (oven-dry) biomass of hardwood species for all live trees on woodland by diameter class, California, 1990s

Species	Diameter class (inches at breast height)											All classes	
	1.0-4.9	5.0-8.9	9.0-12.9	13.0-16.9	17.0-20.9	21.0-24.9	25.0-28.9	29.0-32.9	33.0-36.9	37.0-40.9	41.0+	Total	SE %
	——————————————————————————————— Thousand tons ———————————————————————————————												
Oak group:													
Blue oak	1,962.8	9,778.1	14,257.3	8,666.6	7,023.2	4,641.7	2,798.0	1,401.5	213.1	356.1	—	51,098.5	6
California black oak	464.6	2,348.9	2,716.8	2,593.3	1,678.9	1,374.9	934.4	353.3	394.3	274.3	208.0	13,341.6	11
Canyon live oak	2,707.5	10,080.4	8,893.2	5,341.3	3,037.7	1,941.1	1,309.3	1,201.6	644.9	335.9	1,723.7	37,216.7	10
Coast live oak	431.3	3,737.6	8,295.2	12,672.5	10,503.3	5,616.4	3,891.3	2,837.4	2,316.2	852.1	653.5	51,806.8	11
Engelmann oak	108.3	188.3	134.5	292.6	65.7	531.8	198.9	263.6	—	—	—	1,783.6	50
Interior live oak	5,569.6	10,174.4	6,023.3	3,147.6	2,195.7	820.3	287.9	587.5	82.2	60.7	318.4	29,267.8	12
Oregon white oak	667.7	3,066.0	2,395.2	1,473.8	1,326.3	605.5	328.1	416.9	223.8	213.2	188.4	10,904.7	17
Valley oak	11.1	91.3	1,204.1	652.3	737.1	479.9	872.7	871.7	819.1	216.3	809.2	6,765.0	21
Total	11,922.8	39,465.1	43,919.6	34,839.9	26,567.9	16,011.6	10,620.5	7,933.5	4,693.8	2,308.6	3,901.2	202,184.6	4
Non-oak group:													
Bigleaf maple	83.2	580.6	451.0	349.9	303.2	133.4	66.3	92.2	56.1	93.9	139.5	2,349.2	26
Black cottonwood	—	—	1.3	—	2.8	2.0	—	—	—	—	181.3	185.3	98
California buckeye	165.1	750.8	347.7	225.8	—	—	—	—	—	—	—	1,491.5	20
California laurel	503.0	1,324.3	1,164.3	884.2	436.2	289.8	378.2	—	—	—	—	4,980.1	27
California sycamore	26.1	102.0	14.8	229.9	50.7	304.4	202.5	75.9	79.5	—	—	1,085.7	42
Eucalyptus	36.3	629.2	1,037.2	575.7	819.6	520.7	—	—	—	188.6	—	3,807.3	93
Giant chinquapin	—	—	—	26.5	—	—	—	—	—	—	—	26.5	100
Oregon ash	6.9	63.6	15.4	40.2	24.1	9.3	11.6	—	—	—	—	171.1	71
Pacific madrone	270.9	827.4	2,252.8	784.1	390.4	309.7	289.1	81.8	—	—	—	5,206.3	26
Quaking aspen	82.6	63.1	—	—	21.6	—	—	11.7	—	—	—	179.0	79
Red alder	.5	9.2	—	—	—	—	—	—	—	—	—	9.7	95
Tanoak	31.7	56.0	48.0	28.3	107.3	78.5	76.6	13.1	9.2	—	—	448.6	64
White alder	25.0	25.8	107.8	63.0	36.1	26.7	4.9	46.6	—	—	55.5	391.5	40
Willow	36.2	116.9	182.7	70.7	78.4	125.2	76.1	—	—	—	—	686.2	58
Other hardwoods [a]	45.3	194.5	115.4	137.3	74.8	35.9	21.6	—	—	43.1	—	667.8	42
Total	1,312.8	4,743.3	5,738.4	3,415.7	2,345.1	1,835.6	1,126.9	321.3	144.8	325.6	376.3	21,685.9	18
Total, California	13,235.7	44,208.4	49,658.0	38,255.6	28,913.0	17,847.2	11,747.4	8,254.8	4,838.5	2,634.2	4,277.5	223,870.4	4
SE for total (%)	9	6	5	6	6	8	9	11	17	22	21		4

Note: Excludes reserved lands outside of national forests because these areas were not sampled.

Includes sound and rotten cull trees.

Excludes foliage and dead branches.

SE= sampling error.

— = less than 50 tons.

[a] Other hardwoods includes apple, walnut, and unknowns.

Table 8—Aboveground (oven-dry) biomass of hardwood species for all live trees on timberland by diameter class, California, 1990s

Species	Diameter class (inches at breast height)											All classes	
	1.0-4.9	5.0-8.9	9.0-12.9	13.0-16.9	17.0-20.9	21.0-24.9	25.0-28.9	29.0-32.9	33.0-36.9	37.0-40.9	41.0+	Total	SE
	------------------------------ Thousand tons ------------------------------												%
Oak group:													
Blue oak	3.1	31.9	—	44.7	90.1	29.5	—	—	—	—	73.5	272.8	51
California black oak	2,584.6	12,016.5	14,966.6	12,534.2	9,342.2	8,283.2	5,518.0	4,587.1	2,499.8	1,597.8	2,478.8	76,408.8	4
Canyon live oak	4,397.8	16,478.6	16,932.9	11,308.1	8,177.6	5,924.6	3,721.5	2,911.6	1,959.5	1,296.9	1,480.5	74,589.6	6
Coast live oak	63.8	632.6	1,341.4	1,545.6	1,741.8	815.7	630.5	169.8	67.4	222.7	—	7,231.3	33
Interior live oak	640.4	993.7	671.7	607.9	514.4	431.1	158.7	109.0	116.9	179.9	60.4	4,484.1	18
Oregon white oak	701.2	3,393.3	2,338.4	1,137.8	975.7	724.6	188.9	196.3	66.1	204.3	144.3	10,070.8	13
Valley oak	53.4	214.1	216.9	115.6	91.8	136.8	163.3	101.6	—	—	—	1,093.4	32
Total	8,444.3	33,760.5	36,467.8	27,293.9	20,933.8	16,345.4	10,380.9	8,075.3	4,709.7	3,501.7	4,237.6	174,150.8	4
Non-oak group:													
Bigleaf maple	449.3	1,356.9	1,338.3	942.9	708.6	453.7	89.1	209.2	24.0	126.4	76.9	5,775.4	12
Black cottonwood	8.5	39.1	18.5	1.2	3.5	91.0	25.4	—	78.9	—	—	266.2	55
California buckeye	15.5	46.0	28.2	—	21.8	—	—	—	—	—	—	111.4	38
California laurel	822.3	2,154.0	2,040.9	1,779.1	801.8	561.1	228.7	181.9	139.2	—	63.0	8,771.8	14
Eucalyptus	.4	.7	—	—	—	181.3	103.0	77.2	—	—	328.5	691.0	68
Giant chinquapin	134.5	377.2	452.7	360.7	222.3	101.7	166.2	62.5	—	—	—	1,877.8	22
Oregon ash	20.5	6.8	29.9	46.0	—	—	—	—	15.1	—	—	118.3	53
Pacific dogwood	383.5	76.1	107.4	—	17.6	—	—	—	—	—	—	584.6	17
Pacific madrone	1,412.9	6,115.0	7,942.1	9,267.4	7,138.9	5,058.6	3,486.9	1,822.8	1,267.9	981.5	1,646.8	46,140.7	6
Quaking aspen	57.9	108.1	257.5	334.1	70.5	187.4	3.1	—	7.6	—	—	1,026.2	37
Red alder	336.0	1,305.4	1,877.4	820.2	349.1	230.3	153.9	77.4	51.9	—	89.9	5,291.5	18
Tanoak	7,766.9	19,163.3	19,440.8	13,466.3	10,193.3	6,069.5	3,636.4	2,229.8	691.3	202.8	691.0	83,551.5	6
White alder	64.6	189.8	255.8	326.4	263.8	114.4	77.5	4.4	32.2	31.1	—	1,360.0	22
Willow	52.8	71.9	84.1	40.6	11.7	—	—	—	—	—	—	261.1	33
Other hardwoods[a]	61.4	84.4	96.1	62.7	74.2	121.0	117.1	9.0	15.3	6.1	40.7	687.9	36
Total	11,587.0	31,094.7	33,969.5	27,447.7	19,855.2	13,191.6	8,087.2	4,674.1	2,323.4	1,348.0	2,936.9	156,515.2	4
Total, California	20,031.3	64,855.2	70,437.3	54,741.7	40,788.9	29,537.0	18,468.0	12,749.5	7,033.1	4,849.7	7,174.5	330,666.0	4
SE for total (%)	4	4	4	4	5	5	6	7	10	12	13	3	

Note: Excludes reserved lands outside of national forests because these areas were not sampled.

Includes sound and rotten cull trees.

Excludes foliage and dead branches.

SE= sampling error.

— = less than 50 tons.

[a] Other hardwoods includes apple, walnut, and unknowns.

Table 9—Aboveground (oven-dry) biomass of hardwood species for live trees on woodland and timberland by diameter class, California, 1990s

Species	Diameter class (inches at breast height)											All classes	
	1.0-4.9	5.0-8.9	9.0-12.9	13.0-16.9	17.0-20.9	21.0-24.9	25.0-28.9	29.0-32.9	33.0-36.9	37.0-40.9	41.0+	Total	SE
	Thousand tons												*%*
Oak group:													
Blue oak	1,965.9	9,810.0	14,257.3	8,711.3	7,113.3	4,671.2	2,798.0	1,401.5	213.1	356.1	73.5	51,371.3	6
California black oak	3,049.1	14,365.4	17,683.4	15,127.4	11,021.1	9,658.1	6,452.4	4,940.4	2,894.2	1,872.1	2,686.8	89,750.4	4
Canyon live oak	7,105.3	26,559.0	25,826.1	16,649.4	11,215.3	7,865.7	5,030.8	4,113.2	2,604.4	1,632.8	3,204.2	111,806.3	5
Coast live oak	495.1	4,370.2	9,636.6	14,218.2	12,245.1	6,432.0	4,521.8	3,007.2	2,383.7	1,074.8	653.5	59,038.1	11
Engelmann oak	108.3	188.3	134.5	292.6	65.7	531.8	198.9	263.6	—	—	—	1,783.6	50
Interior live oak	6,210.0	11,168.1	6,695.0	3,755.5	2,710.1	1,251.5	446.6	696.5	199.1	240.5	378.8	33,751.8	11
Oregon white oak	1,368.9	6,459.2	4,733.6	2,611.5	2,302.0	1,330.1	517.0	613.1	289.9	417.5	332.7	20,975.5	11
Valley oak	64.5	305.4	1,420.9	767.9	828.9	616.6	1,036.0	973.3	819.1	216.3	809.2	7,858.4	19
Total	20,367.1	73,225.6	80,387.4	62,133.8	47,501.7	32,357.0	21,001.4	16,008.8	9,403.5	5,810.2	8,138.8	376,335.4	3
Non-oak group:													
Bigleaf maple	532.5	1,937.5	1,789.3	1,292.8	1,011.8	587.1	155.4	301.4	80.1	220.4	216.5	8,124.7	11
Black cottonwood	8.5	39.1	19.8	1.2	6.3	91.0	25.4	—	78.9	—	181.3	451.5	52
California buckeye	180.6	796.9	375.9	225.8	—	23.8	—	—	—	—	—	1,602.9	19
California laurel	1,325.2	3,478.3	3,205.2	2,663.3	1,238.0	850.9	606.8	181.9	139.2	—	63.0	13,751.8	13
California sycamore	26.1	102.0	14.8	229.9	50.7	304.4	202.5	75.9	79.5	—	—	1,085.7	42
Eucalyptus	36.7	629.8	1,037.2	575.7	819.6	702.0	103.0	77.2	—	188.6	328.5	4,498.3	78
Giant chinquapin	134.5	377.2	452.7	387.2	222.3	101.7	166.2	62.5	—	—	—	1,904.3	22
Oregon ash	27.4	70.4	45.2	86.2	24.1	9.3	11.6	—	15.1	—	—	289.4	47
Pacific dogwood	383.5	76.1	107.4	—	17.6	—	—	—	—	—	—	584.6	17
Pacific madrone	1,683.8	6,942.3	10,194.9	10,051.6	7,529.3	5,368.2	3,776.0	1,904.6	1,267.9	981.5	1,646.8	51,347.0	6
Quaking aspen	140.4	171.3	257.5	334.1	92.1	187.4	3.1	11.7	7.6	—	—	1,205.2	34
Red alder	336.5	1,314.6	1,877.4	820.2	349.1	230.3	153.9	77.4	51.9	89.9	—	5,301.2	18
Tanoak	7,798.6	19,219.3	19,488.9	13,494.6	10,300.6	6,148.0	3,712.9	2,242.9	700.5	202.8	691.0	84,000.1	6
White alder	89.6	215.6	363.5	389.4	299.9	141.1	82.4	50.9	32.2	31.1	55.5	1,751.4	19
Willow	89.0	188.9	266.8	111.3	90.1	125.2	76.1	—	—	—	—	947.3	43
Other hardwoods[a]	106.7	278.9	211.4	200.1	148.9	156.9	138.6	9.0	15.3	49.3	40.7	1,355.8	28
Total	12,899.9	35,838.1	39,707.9	30,863.6	22,200.3	15,027.2	9,214.1	4,995.4	2,468.2	1,673.6	3,313.2	178,201.1	4
Total, California	33,267.0	109,063.7	120,095.3	92,997.4	69,702.0	47,384.1	30,215.5	21,004.2	11,871.7	7,483.9	11,452.0	554,536.6	2
SE for total (%)	4	3	3	3	4	4	5	6	9	11	11	2	

Note: Excludes reserved lands outside of national forests because these areas were not sampled.

Includes sound and rotten cull trees.

Excludes foliage and dead branches.

SE= sampling error.

— = less than 50 tons.

[a] Other hardwoods includes apple, walnut, and unknowns.

Table 10—Total stem volume of hardwood species (≥4 inches diameter at breast height) on unreserved woodland and timberland by resource area and owner, California, 1990s

Resource area and species	Woodland National forest	Other public	Private	Total Volume	SE	Timberland National forest	Other public	Private	Total Volume	SE	Total National forest	Other public	Private	Total Volume	SE
	Million cubic feet				*%*	*Million cubic feet*				*%*	*Million cubic feet*				*%*
North Coast:															
Oak group—															
Blue oak	—	—	53.1	53.1	54	—	—	—	—	—	—	—	53.1	53.1	54
California black oak	23.3	—	138.6	161.9	21	47.6	41.0	391.4	479.9	14	70.8	41.0	530.0	641.7	12
Canyon live oak	74.9	0.3	80.0	155.2	37	109.6	55.7	274.0	439.3	17	184.5	56.0	354.0	594.5	16
Coast live oak	—	10.2	129.8	140.0	32	—	—	55.8	55.8	38	—	10.2	185.6	195.8	26
Interior live oak	—	—	23.8	23.8	55	4.4	3.8	45.1	53.3	41	4.4	3.8	68.8	77.1	33
Oregon white oak	65.9	7.3	255.6	328.7	24	4.8	8.7	311.4	324.9	18	70.7	16.0	567.0	653.6	15
Valley oak	—	—	48.7	48.7	48	—	—	41.3	41.3	43	—	—	89.9	89.9	33
Total	164.1	17.8	729.5	911.3		166.4	109.1	1,118.9	1,394.4		330.4	126.9	1,848.3	2,305.6	
Non-oak group—															
Bigleaf maple	4.4	—	17.1	21.5	57	33.4	6.1	98.7	138.2	21	37.8	6.1	115.8	159.7	20
Black cottonwood	—	—	—	—		—	—	7.2	7.2	92	—	—	7.2	7.2	92
California buckeye	.5	—	16.2	16.8	56	—	—	1.9	1.9	74	.5	—	18.1	18.6	52
California laurel	.5	—	95.8	96.3	47	10.2	9.1	294.2	313.5	15	10.7	9.1	390.0	409.8	17
Eucalyptus	—	—	—	—		—	—	16.5	16.5	81	—	—	16.5	16.5	81
Giant chinquapin	—	—	—	—		39.8	—	29.7	69.5	34	39.8	—	29.7	69.5	34
Oregon ash	—	—	—	—		—	—	1.9	1.9	99	—	—	1.9	1.9	99
Pacific dogwood	—	—	—	—		.6	—	1.5	2.1	53	.6	—	1.5	2.1	53
Pacific madrone	11.7	4.5	95.4	111.6	34	178.1	73.6	917.4	1,169.1	9	189.9	78.1	1,012.8	1,280.7	9
Red alder	—	—	—	—		2.8	—	242.7	245.4	22	2.8	—	242.7	245.4	22
Tanoak	—	—	—	—		517.5	66.3	2,752.0	3,335.8	7	517.5	66.3	2,752.0	3,335.8	7
White alder	—	—	—	—		1.2	—	—	1.2	75	1.2	—	—	1.2	75
Willow	—	—	—	—		—	—	11.7	11.7	51	—	—	11.7	11.7	51
Total	17.2	4.5	224.5	246.1		783.7	155.1	4,375.2	5,314.0		800.9	159.6	4,599.6	5,560.1	
Total, North Coast	181.2	22.3	953.9	1,157.4	11	950.1	264.2	5,494.0	6,708.3	5	1,131.3	286.5	6,447.9	7,865.7	4
SE for total (%)	34	58	12	11		20	22	5	5		17	21	5	4	

79

Table 10—Total stem volume of hardwood species (≥4 inches diameter at breast height) on unreserved woodland and timberland by resource area and owner, California, 1990s (continued)

Resource area and species	Woodland					Timberland					Total				
	National forest	Other public	Private	Total Volume	SE %	National forest	Other public	Private	Total Volume	SE %	National forest	Other public	Private	Total Volume	SE %
	Million cubic feet					*Million cubic feet*					*Million cubic feet*				
North Interior:															
Oak group—															
Blue oak	3.0	6.8	191.5	201.3	22	2.5	—	—	2.5	100	5.5	6.8	191.5	203.7	21
California black oak	77.3	7.4	61.4	146.1	24	505.4	47.5	554.6	1,107.5	8	582.7	54.9	615.9	1,253.5	7
Canyon live oak	165.4	29.5	29.9	224.8	25	638.3	54.8	316.9	1,010.0	11	803.7	84.3	346.8	1,234.8	10
Coast live oak	—	—	—	—	100	.4	—	—	.4	100	.4	—	—	.4	100
Interior live oak	17.8	—	34.0	51.8	40	31.1	—	.8	31.9	33	49.0	—	34.8	83.7	27
Oregon white oak	46.8	24.2	90.8	161.8	26	53.9	19.2	66.5	139.6	19	100.7	43.4	157.3	301.4	16
Valley oak	1.1	1.3	29.5	31.9	53	4.5	—	1.0	5.5	39	5.5	1.3	30.5	37.4	46
Total	311.3	69.2	437.0	817.6		1,236.2	121.5	939.7	2,297.4		1,547.5	190.7	1,376.7	3,114.9	
Non-oak group—															
Bigleaf maple	30.2	—	3.1	33.4	57	85.8	7.2	59.3	152.3	20	116.1	7.2	62.4	185.7	19
Black cottonwood	—	—	9.8	9.8	100	.1	1.9	—	1.9	97	.1	1.9	9.8	11.8	85
California buckeye	.4	—	.8	1.1	75	.4	—	—	.4	100	.8	—	.8	1.6	61
California laurel	—	—	—	—		2.8	1.0	12.6	16.4	66	2.8	1.0	12.6	16.4	66
Eucalyptus	—	—	—	—		—	—	—	—	100	—	—	—	—	100
Giant chinquapin	1.8	—	—	1.8	100	29.1	—	6.2	35.3	32	30.9	—	6.2	37.0	30
Oregon ash	—	—	—	—		1.0	—	—	1.0	100	1.0	—	—	1.0	100
Pacific dogwood	—	—	—	—		2.9	—	.3	3.2	53	2.9	—	.3	3.2	53
Pacific madrone	28.4	—	2.5	30.9	76	362.9	—	53.3	416.2	12	391.4	—	55.8	447.1	13
Quaking aspen	—	—	—	—		27.9	—	12.4	40.3	54	27.9	—	12.4	40.3	54
Red alder	.5	—	—	.5	100	14.4	—	—	14.4	39	14.8	—	—	14.8	38
Tanoak	7.0	—	—	7.0	100	228.9	—	48.6	277.5	23	235.9	—	48.6	284.4	23
White alder	.7	—	—	.7	100	7.1	—	10.4	17.6	45	7.8	—	10.4	18.3	43
Willow	—	—	—	—		—	—	.8	.8	100	—	—	.8	.8	100
Other hardwoods[a]	1.1	—	—	1.1	100	3.8	—	—	3.8	100	4.9	—	—	4.9	100
Total	70.0	—	16.2	86.2		767.1	10.0	203.9	981.1		832.3	10.0	220.1	1,061.5	
Total, North Interior	381.3	69.2	453.2	903.7		2,003.3	131.5	1,143.6	3,278.4		2,379.8	200.8	1,596.7	4,176.4	
SE for total (%)	21	44	14	12		7	31	9	6		7	26	8	5	

Table 10—Total stem volume of hardwood species (≥4 inches diameter at breast height) on unreserved woodland and timberland by resource area and owner, California, 1990s (continued)

Resource area and species	Woodland National forest	Woodland Other public	Woodland Private	Woodland Total Volume	Woodland SE %	Timberland National forest	Timberland Other public	Timberland Private	Timberland Total Volume	Timberland SE %	Total National forest	Total Other public	Total Private	Total Volume	Total SE %
	— — — — Million cubic feet — — — —					*— — — — Million cubic feet — — — —*					*— — — — Million cubic feet — — — —*				
Sacramento:															
Oak group—															
Blue oak	0.3	18.3	822.2	840.9	11	—	—	3.5	3.5	100	0.3	18.3	825.7	844.3	11
California black oak	85.9	—	123.0	208.9	21	627.0	22.3	781.9	1,431.3	8	712.9	22.3	904.9	1,640.2	7
Canyon live oak	182.0	26.7	102.6	311.4	22	312.2	47.5	216.3	576.0	14	494.2	74.3	318.9	887.4	12
Interior live oak	—	5.0	195.9	200.9	23	6.2	.2	35.4	41.8	35	6.2	5.2	231.2	242.7	20
Oregon white oak	1.1	—	—	1.1	100	1.4	—	.7	2.2	74	2.6	—	.7	3.3	59
Valley oak	4.0	—	64.9	69.0	64	—	—	.2	.2	100	4.0	—	65.2	69.2	63
Total	273.4	50.1	1,308.7	1,632.1		946.9	70.0	1,038.0	2,054.9		1,220.2	120.1	2,346.7	3,687.1	
Non-oak group—															
Bigleaf maple	8.6	—	18.5	27.1	48	13.2	—	45.9	59.1	25	21.8	—	64.4	86.2	23
Black cottonwood	—	—	—	—		—	—	5.5	5.5	81	—	—	5.5	5.5	81
California buckeye	3.5	—	13.3	16.8	44	2.4	—	.2	2.6	73	5.8	—	13.5	19.4	39
California laurel	.7	—	—	.7	65	5.8	.5	17.6	23.8	49	6.4	.5	17.6	24.5	48
California sycamore	.2	—	—	.2	100	—	—	—	—		.2	—	—	.2	100
Oregon ash	.3	—	—	.3	100	—	—	—	—		.3	—	—	.3	100
Pacific dogwood	—	—	—	—		1.3	—	—	1.3	89	1.3	—	—	1.3	89
Pacific madrone	.7	—	—	.7	61	52.1	2.3	82.4	136.8	20	52.8	2.3	82.4	137.6	20
Quaking aspen	.2	—	—	.2	100	1.9	—	2.4	4.3	63	2.1	—	2.4	4.5	61
Red alder	—	—	—	—		2.6	—	11.6	14.2	54	2.6	—	11.6	14.2	54
Tanoak	—	—	—	—		71.3	.1	103.6	175.0	21	71.3	.1	103.6	175.0	21
White alder	1.0	—	—	1.0	100	1.8	—	13.2	15.0	49	2.9	—	13.2	16.0	47
Willow	—	—	14.7	14.7	100	—	—	1.3	1.3	100	—	—	16.0	16.0	92
Other hardwoods[a]	.2	—	—	.2	100	.7	—	1.2	1.8	100	.9	—	1.2	2.0	100
Total	15.3	—	46.5	61.8		153.0	2.9	284.9	440.8		168.4	2.9	331.4	502.6	
Total, Sacramento	288.7	50.1	1,355.2	1,694.0	8	1,099.9	72.9	1,322.9	2,495.7	6	1,388.6	123.0	2,678.1	4,189.7	5
SE for total (%)	14	34	10			8	25	10			7	20	7		

Table 10—Total stem volume of hardwood species (≥4 inches diameter at breast height) on unreserved woodland and timberland by resource area and owner, California, 1990s (continued)

Resource area and species	Woodland					Timberland					Total				
	National forest	Other public	Private	Total Volume	SE %	National forest	Other public	Private	Total Volume	SE %	National forest	Other public	Private	Total Volume	SE %
	Million cubic feet					*Million cubic feet*					*Million cubic feet*				
Central Coast:															
Oak group—															
Blue oak	47.4	67.0	452.5	566.9	13	—	—	5.5	5.5	100	47.4	67.0	458.0	572.4	13
California black oak	—	—	20.7	20.7	63	9.0	—	2.7	11.6	58	9.0	—	23.4	32.3	45
Canyon live oak	3.4	—	9.5	12.9	74	28.1	—	62.4	90.5	71	31.5	—	71.9	103.4	63
Coast live oak	83.3	94.6	1,304.5	1,482.3	13	2.6	—	203.9	206.4	44	85.8	94.6	1,508.4	1,688.8	13
Interior live oak	.5	—	50.7	51.2	95	3.3	—	—	3.3	93	3.8	—	50.7	54.5	89
Oregon white oak	—	—	32.1	32.1	63	—	—	2.0	2.0	101	—	—	34.1	34.1	59
Valley oak	—	—	149.9	149.9	33	—	—	—	—		—	—	149.9	149.9	33
Total	134.5	161.6	2,019.8	2,315.9		42.9	—	276.5	319.4		177.4	161.6	2,296.3	2,635.3	
Non-oak group—															
Bigleaf maple	3.8	—	35.9	39.7	71	—	—	4.1	4.1	65	3.8	—	40.0	43.8	65
California buckeye	—	—	9.7	9.7	51	—	—	—	—		—	—	9.7	9.7	51
California laurel	1.0	7.7	122.4	131.1	38	1.2	—	67.8	68.9	58	2.2	7.7	190.1	200.0	32
California sycamore	4.4	16.9	40.0	61.3	41	—	—	—	—		4.4	16.9	40.0	61.3	41
Eucalyptus	—	—	106.7	106.7	100	—	—	4.5	4.5	100	—	—	111.2	111.2	96
Pacific madrone	3.1	35.3	31.8	70.1	61	6.6	—	93.9	100.5	31	9.7	35.3	125.6	170.6	30
Tanoak	—	—	—	—		3.7	—	260.4	264.1	35	3.7	—	260.4	264.1	35
Willow	—	—	24.9	24.9	100	—	—	2.9	2.9	90	—	—	27.8	27.8	89
Other hardwoods[a]	4.4	—	—	4.4	100	16.8	—	—	16.8	100	21.2	—	—	21.2	100
Total	16.7	59.9	371.2	447.8		28.3	—	433.5	461.9		45.0	59.9	804.7	909.7	
Total, Central Coast	151.2	221.5	2,391.1	2,763.7		71.2	—	710.0	781.2		222.4	221.5	3,101.0	3,544.9	
SE for total (%)	27	32	10	9		31	—	17	16		20	32	9	8	

Table 10—Total stem volume of hardwood species (≥4 inches diameter at breast height) on unreserved woodland and timberland by resource area and owner, California, 1990s (continued)

Resource area and species	Woodland					Timberland					Total				
	National forest	Other public	Private	Total Volume	SE %	National forest	Other public	Private	Total Volume	SE %	National forest	Other public	Private	Total Volume	SE %
	Million cubic feet					*Million cubic feet*					*Million cubic feet*				
Southern:															
Oak group—															
Blue oak	42.9	37.5	812.1	892.6	10	0.6	—	—	.6	100	43.5	37.5	812.1	893.2	10
California black oak	86.8	12.3	11.7	110.7	28	388.2	16.4	287.2	691.8	10	475.0	28.7	298.8	802.5	9
Canyon live oak	245.6	30.4	136.9	412.9	19	178.2	27.8	155.8	361.8	16	423.9	58.2	292.7	774.7	13
Coast live oak	72.3	30.4	95.2	197.9	16	1.3	—	6.6	7.9	74	73.6	30.4	101.9	205.8	15
Engelmann oak	—	—	93.4	93.4	50	—	—	—	—		—	—	93.4	93.4	50
Interior live oak	52.5	47.3	517.6	617.5	17	6.3	—	7.0	13.2	38	58.8	47.3	524.6	630.7	16
Oregon white oak	—	—	18.4	18.4	100	—	—	.4	.4	100	—	—	18.8	18.8	98
Valley oak	.2	—	29.6	29.8	53	—	—	10.4	10.4	53	.2	—	40.0	40.2	42
Total	500.3	157.9	1,714.9	2,373.1		574.6	44.2	467.4	1,086.2		1,074.9	202.0	2,182.3	3,459.3	
Non-oak group—															
Bigleaf maple	8.7	—	—	8.7	66	8.7	—	3.0	11.7	40	17.5	—	3.0	20.5	36
Black cottonwood	.2	—	—	.2	75	—	—	—	—		.2	—	—	.2	75
California buckeye	13.7	12.4	42.4	68.5	28	2.2	—	—	2.2	100	15.9	12.4	42.4	70.8	28
California laurel	6.1	—	—	6.1	52	.2	.5	2.0	2.7	77	6.3	.5	2.0	8.8	43
California sycamore	1.2	—	—	1.2	55	—	—	—	—		1.2	—	—	1.2	55
Eucalyptus	—	—	11.1	11.1	100	—	—	—	—		—	—	11.1	11.1	100
Oregon ash	6.9	—	3.3	10.2	73	1.1	2.3	.2	3.5	72	8.0	2.3	3.5	13.7	58
Pacific dogwood	—	—	—	—		1.1	—	3.6	4.7	50	1.1	—	3.6	4.7	50
Pacific madrone	—	—	—	—		—	—	2.8	2.8	101	—	—	2.8	2.8	101
Quaking aspen	5.0	—	—	5.0	100	2.9	—	3.2	6.2	60	8.0	—	3.2	11.2	56
Red alder	—	—	—	—		.8	—	—	.8	100	.8	—	—	.8	100
Tanoak	—	—	—	—		—	—	1.4	1.4	75	—	—	1.4	1.4	75
Walnut	—	—	—	—		—	—	3.3	3.3	100	—	—	3.3	3.3	100
White alder	7.6	—	3.6	11.2	46	14.0	—	13.9	27.8	34	21.6	—	17.5	39.0	28
Willow	—	—	20.7	20.7	100	—	—	2.8	2.8	100	—	—	23.5	23.5	90
Other hardwoods[a]	23.1	—	—	23.1	100	5.3	—	—	5.3	100	28.4	—	—	28.4	100
Total	72.6	12.4	81.2	166.1		36.4	2.8	36.1	75.2		108.9	15.2	117.3	241.3	
Total, Southern	572.9	170.2	1,796.1	2,539.2		611.0	47.0	503.5	1,161.4		1,183.9	217.2	2,299.5	3,700.6	
SE for total (%)	9	30	8	6		9	33	17	9		6	26	7	5	

83

Table 10—Total stem volume of hardwood species (≥4 inches diameter at breast height) on unreserved woodland and timberland by resource area and owner, California, 1990s (continued)

Resource area and species	Woodland National forest	Other public	Private	Total Volume	SE %	Timberland National forest	Other public	Private	Total Volume	SE %	Total National forest	Other public	Private	Total Volume	SE %
	— — — — — Million cubic feet — — — — —					*— — — — — Million cubic feet — — — — —*					*— — — — — Million cubic feet — — — — —*				
Total, California:															
Oak group—															
Blue oak	93.6	129.7	2,331.4	2,554.6	6	3.1	—	9.0	12.1	58	96.7	129.7	2,340.4	2,566.7	6
California black oak	273.2	19.7	355.3	648.2	11	1,577.2	127.2	2,017.7	3,722.1	5	1,850.4	146.9	2,373.0	4,370.3	4
Canyon live oak	671.3	86.9	358.9	1,117.2	12	1,266.4	185.8	1,025.4	2,477.6	7	1,937.7	272.7	1,384.3	3,594.7	6
Coast live oak	155.5	135.1	1,529.5	1,820.2	11	4.3	—	266.3	270.5	35	159.8	135.1	1,795.8	2,090.7	11
Engelmann oak	—	—	93.4	93.4	50	—	—	—	—		—	—	93.4	93.4	50
Interior live oak	70.8	52.4	821.9	945.1	13	51.4	4.0	88.2	143.6	20	122.2	56.4	910.1	1,088.6	12
Oregon white oak	113.8	31.5	396.8	542.1	18	60.2	27.9	381.0	469.1	13	173.9	59.4	777.8	1,011.2	12
Valley oak	5.3	1.3	322.5	329.1	22	4.5	—	53.0	57.4	32	9.8	1.3	375.5	386.5	20
Total	1,383.5	456.5	6,209.8	8,049.9		2,966.9	344.9	3,840.5	7,152.3		4,350.5	801.4	10,050.3	15,202.1	
Non-oak group—															
Bigleaf maple	55.7	—	74.7	130.4	29	141.2	13.3	210.9	365.4	12	196.9	13.3	285.6	495.8	12
Black cottonwood	.2	—	9.8	10.1	98	.1	1.9	12.7	14.6	57	.3	1.9	22.5	24.7	53
California buckeye	18.1	12.4	82.4	112.9	21	5.0	—	2.1	7.1	46	23.1	12.4	84.5	120.0	20
California laurel	8.4	7.7	218.1	234.2	29	20.1	11.1	394.2	425.3	15	28.4	18.8	612.3	659.5	14
California sycamore	5.8	16.9	40.0	62.7	40	—	—	21.0	21.1	67	5.8	16.9	40.0	62.7	40
Eucalyptus	—	—	117.8	117.8	94	—	—	—	—		—	—	138.8	138.9	79
Giant chinquapin	1.8	—	—	1.8	100	68.9	—	35.8	104.7	25	70.7	—	35.8	106.5	25
Oregon ash	7.2	—	3.3	10.5	71	2.1	2.3	2.1	6.4	52	9.3	2.3	5.4	17.0	48
Pacific dogwood	—	—	—	—		6.0	—	5.4	11.3	29	6.0	—	5.4	11.3	29
Pacific madrone	44.0	39.8	129.6	213.3	28	599.8	75.9	1,149.7	1,825.5	7	643.8	115.7	1,279.3	2,038.8	7
Quaking aspen	5.2	—	—	5.2	96	32.7	—	18.1	50.8	44	37.9	—	18.1	56.0	41
Red alder	.5	—	—	.5	100	20.6	—	254.2	274.8	20	21.0	—	254.2	275.2	20
Tanoak	7.0	—	—	7.0	100	821.4	66.4	3,165.9	4,053.7	6	828.4	66.4	3,165.9	4,060.7	6
Walnut	—	—	—	—		—	—	3.3	3.3	100	—	—	3.3	3.3	100
White alder	9.3	—	3.6	12.9	41	24.1	—	37.4	61.5	23	33.4	—	41.0	74.4	21
Willow	—	—	60.2	60.2	59	—	—	19.6	19.6	37	—	—	79.8	79.9	45
Other hardwoods[a]	28.7	—	—	28.7	100	26.6	—	1.2	27.8	100	55.3	—	1.2	56.5	100
Total	191.8	76.8	739.5	1,008.1		1,768.6	170.8	5,333.5	7,272.9		1,960.3	247.6	6,073.0	8,280.9	
Total, California	1,575.3	533.3	6,949.3	9,057.9	4	4,735.5	515.6	9,174.0	14,425.1	3	6,310.8	1,049.0	16,123.3	23,483.1	2
SE for total (%)	8	18	5	4		5	14	4	3		4	11	3	2	

Note: Excludes rotten cull trees.

Volume is for the total stem of live trees from the ground to the tree tip.

SE = sampling error.

— = less than 50,000 cubic feet.

[a] Other hardwoods includes apple and unknowns.

Table 11—Forest type area 1984 and 1994 by owner, on unreserved woodland outside national forests, California

Forest type	1984 Other public	1984 Private	1984 Total	1994 Other public	1994 Private	1994 Total
			Thousand acres			
Oak group:						
Blue oak	178.1	2,855.3	3,033.4	157.9	2,708.7	2,866.6
California black oak	—	223.1	223.1	12.7	181.0	193.7
Canyon live oak	47.6	184.2	231.8	47.6	164.4	212.1
Coast live oak	93.7	854.8	948.5	60.7	836.1	896.8
Engelmann oak	—	56.3	56.3	—	75.1	75.1
Interior live oak	64.7	781.3	846.0	80.9	805.1	886.1
Oregon white oak	47.6	223.1	270.7	47.6	223.1	270.7
Valley oak	16.3	102.2	118.5	—	118.7	118.7
Total	448.2	5,280.2	5,728.4	407.5	5,112.1	5,519.6
Non-oak group:						
Bigleaf maple	—	16.3	16.3	—	16.3	16.3
Buckeye	—	64.7	64.7	—	80.9	80.9
California laurel	—	34.8	34.8	—	34.8	34.8
Eucalyptus	—	37.3	37.3	—	18.5	18.5
Oregon ash	—	16.3	16.3	—	16.3	16.3
Pacific madrone	—	51.2	51.2	—	51.2	51.2
Sycamore	16.6	—	16.6	16.6	—	16.6
Walnut	—	—	—	—	18.8	18.8
White alder	—	—	—	—	16.2	16.2
Willow	—	16.2	16.2	—	16.2	16.2
Total	16.6	236.8	253.4	16.6	269.2	285.8
Total, California	464.8	5,517.1	5,981.9	424.2	5,381.2	5,805.4

Note: Includes area reductions caused by the transfer of land to reserved status or national forest ownership.

Forest type is determined by applying a classification algorithm to trees. For this table, some tree measurements for 1984 were derived by backdating 1994 tree measurements, via models or other standard protocol.

— = less than 50 acres.

Table 12—Change in forest type area from 1984 to 1994 on unreserved woodland and timberland outside of national forests, California

Forest type	1984 hardwood forest type area (A)	Changed status to reserved or national forest (B)	1984 hardwoods forest type area, adjusted[a] (C)	Changed to a different hardwood forest type (D)	Changed to a softwood forest type (E)	Changed to non-stocked (F)	Changed to non-forest (G)	Remained as the same forest type (H)	Changed from a different forest type (I)	1994 hardwood forest type area — Area (J)	SE[b] (K)	Changed proportion from 1984 to 1994, adjusted[a] (L)
	--- Thousands acres ---										%	%
Oak group:												
Blue oak[c]	3,033	-95	2,938	-132			-21	2,784	82	2,867	5	-2
California black oak	751	-37	714	-16	-34	-15		650	15	665	12	-7
Canyon live oak	571	-28	543	-16	-10			517	86	603	14	11
Coast live oak	1,027	-34	993	-35				958		958	10	-4
Engelmann oak	56		56	0				56	19	75	38	33
Interior live oak	902	-9	893	-49				844	115	959	11	7
Oregon white oak	483		483	-6	-18			459	5	464	15	-4
Valley oak	141		141	-16				124	16	141	33	0
Total	6,964	-203	6,761	-271	-62	-15	-21	6,392	339	6,731	2	0
Non-oak group:												
Bigleaf maple	76		76	-7	-8			60		60	43	-20
Buckeye	65		65					65	16	81	44	25
California laurel	113		113	-8				106	25	131	29	16
Pacific madrone	282	-7	275	-8	-23			243	25	267	19	-3
Red alder	49		49		-9			41	30	70	34	42
Tanoak	955	-16	939	-22	-34		-24	859	103	962	8	2
Other hardwoods[d]	132	0	132	-8	-9	0	-25	90	69	159	34	0
Total	1,672	-23	1,648	-53	-82		-49	1,464	268	1,731	6	5
Total, California	8,636	-226	8,410	-325	-144	-15	-70	7,855	606	8,462	2	1

Note: The columns in this table are additive as follows: A + B = C; C + D + E + F + G = H; H + I = J; L = (J - C) / C.

[a] Adjusted columns do not include forest that was in the inventory in the 1980s but was not inventoried in the 1990s owing to a transfer of land to reserve status or national forest ownership. There were no transfers from reserve status or national forest into the 1990s inventory.

[b] The standard error includes sampling error but not measurement error. For estimates in this table, a change in plot design between 1981-84 and 1991-94 contributes to measurement error; some tree measurements for 1981-84 were derived from backdating 1991-94 tree measurements.

[c] The blue oak forest type includes the area of ghost pine (*Pinus sabiniana*) forest type.

[d] Other hardwood forest types included California sycamore, eucalyptus, giant chinquipin, Oregon ash, white alder, walnut, and willow.

Table 13—Net growing-stock volume of hardwood species, 1984 and 1994, on unreserved woodland and timberland outside national forests, California

Species	1984		1994		Change 1994-1984	
	Total	SE	Total	SE	Total	SE
	– – – – – – – – – – –Million cubic feet – – – – – – – – – – –					
Oak group:						
Blue oak	965.2	178.2	1,080.9	205.1	115.6	43.0
California black oak	1,477.7	115.1	1,681.3	130.5	203.5	38.2
Canyon live oak	954.9	162.4	1,080.4	159.5	125.4	57.5
Coast live oak	961.4	326.8	1,063.1	359.3	101.9	57.2
Engelmann oak	10.6	10.6	11.3	11.3	.7	.7
Interior live oak	389.4	154.6	413.0	119.4	23.6	55.7
Oregon white oak	557.4	196.8	671.4	246.2	114.0	51.9
Valley oak	513.2	276.5	600.2	330.8	87.2	61.7
Total	5,829.9	588.7	6,601.5	658.2	772.0	144.7
Non-oak group:						
Bigleaf maple	128.2	23.4	166.1	29.6	38.0	9.3
Black cottonwood	13.8	13.1	14.0	12.5	—	
Buckeye	19.4	10.6	11.5	9.7	-7.9	7.9
California laurel	404.3	114.4	513.7	140.4	109.4	30.2
Eucalyptus	154.2	149.6	197.3	193.8	43.1	43.1
Giant chinquapin	24.4	7.8	30.5	9.7	6.1	6.1
Pacific madrone	1,026.4	120.3	1,162.8	135.8	136.4	30.0
Quaking aspen	5.2	3.2	6.1	3.7	1.0	1.0
Red alder	142.2	33.7	213.0	50.2	70.7	35.4
Sycamore	23.6	23.6	32.4	32.4	8.8	8.8
Tanoak	1,504.3	128.4	1,802.1	136.4	297.9	90.2
Walnut	.7	.7	1.1	1.1	.4	.4
White alder	39.2	17.0	56.6	26.3	17.4	10.6
Total	3,485.8	270.2	4,207.2	321.9	721.4	121.7
Total, California	9,315.8	650.5	10,808.7	736.0	1,493.4	187.0

Note: Excludes cull trees and cull volume; includes trees ≥5inches diameter at breast height. Values for 1994 may differ from those of table 3 because estimates are based only on remeasured plots that were in the inventory in both 1984 and 1994.

This table does not include volume from land that transferred to reserved status or national forest ownership in the 1990s.

SE= sampling error.

— = less than 50,000 cubic feet.

Table 14—Gross volume of periodic mortality, periodic removals, annual mortality, and annual removals for hardwood trees that died during the remeasurement period (1984 to 1994), on unreserved woodland and timberland outside national forests, California

	Periodic mortality		Periodic removals[a]		Annual mortality	Annual removals
	Volume	SE	Volume	SE		
	1000 ft³	%	1000 ft³	%	---- 1000 ft³ ----	
Oak group:						
Blue oak	73,610.1	47	45,182.0	51	6,031.1	3,797.9
California black oak	155,435.0	18	70,954.8	29	13,450.7	5,966.0
Canyon live oak	95,107.8	69	14,795.7	55	8,169.1	1,332.3
Coast live oak	76,484.3	61	15,890.8	93	6,392.7	1,444.7
Interior live oak	9,257.1	79	86,525.1	87	779.4	6,723.5
Oregon white oak	19,626.2	51	3,120.6	68	1,912.7	312.1
Valley oak	28,057.4	97	—		2,565.3	—
Total	457,577.8	23	236,469.0	35	39,300.9	19,576.5
Non-oak group:						
Bigleaf maple	3,791.0	56	4,606.1	80	333.1	460.6
Black cottonwood	2,868.2	100	—		220.6	—
Buckeye	15,603.0	57	281.5	100	1,342.7	28.2
California laurel	13,016.9	41	10,820.6	85	1,227.8	1,087.4
Eucalyptus	19,696.4	93	—		1,534.5	—
Giant chinquapin	2,852.3	73	—		296.1	—
Pacific madrone	71,696.0	24	55,797.8	32	6,826.0	5,558.9
Red alder	12,629.7	41	40,397.2	64	1,254.8	4,001.2
Tanoak	62,500.4	18	252,870.5	25	6,249.8	25,612.0
White alder	2,442.5	79	550.9	100	208.4	45.9
Other hardwoods	12,355.8	69	5,270.4	100	1,049.4	484.3
Total	219,452.3	14	370,594.9	22	20,543.1	37,278.3
Total, California	677,030.1	17	607,063.8	19	59,844.0	56,854.8

Note: Gross volume is the volume of a tree from a 1-foot stump to a 4-inch diameter top, with no deduction for cull sections of rot or poor form.

Includes all hardwood trees ≥5 inches diameter at breast height that were alive in 1981-84 and dead in 1991-94.

Includes sound and rotten cull trees.

Excludes volume from land that transferred to reserved status or national forest ownership in the 1990s.

Excludes volume from land that was converted from forest to developed land, roads, or other types of nonforest in the 1990s.

— = less than 50 cubic feet.

SE = sampling error.

[a] Removals include all trees that were cut or culturally killed during the remeasurement period.

Table 15—Gross volume in 1984 and average annual volume change (1984 to 1994) for hardwood species, on unre-served woodland and timberland outside national forests, California

Species	1984 gross volume		Annual gross growth		Annual mortality and removals		Annual net growth	
	Volume	SE	Volume	SE	Volume	SE	Volume	SE
	Thousand cubic feet							
Oak group:								
Blue oak	1,457,529	250,442	22,737	4,215	9,829	3,336	12,908	4,497
California black oak	1,997,285	156,684	33,692	2,643	19,417	3,079	14,275	3,615
Canyon live oak	1,297,255	247,791	19,630	2,910	9,501	5,541	10,129	5,459
Coast live oak	1,317,764	422,411	22,154	7,182	7,837	4,118	14,317	7,023
Engelmann oak	10,731	10,747	73	73	—	—	73	73
Interior live oak	521,333	178,920	9,034	2,098	7,503	5,778	1,531	4,931
Oregon white oak	704,753	234,744	13,502	5,118	2,225	1,018	11,277	5,155
Valley oak	546,067	282,026	10,394	5,383	2,565	2,410	7,829	5,320
Total	7,852,716	713,645	131,217	12,060	58,877	10,792	72,340	14,179
Non-oak group:								
Bigleaf maple	166,555	29,310	4,218	746	794	413	3,424	801
Black cottonwood	18,268	18,285	275	258	221	221	54	37
Buckeye	133,790	69,868	1,865	761	1,371	765	494	1,017
California laurel	469,997	125,234	12,413	2,844	2,315	1,042	10,097	2,865
Eucalyptus	159,279	154,733	4,796	4,796	1,535	1,414	3,262	3,262
Giant chinquapin	24,635	7,899	751	249	296	223	455	291
Pacific madrone	1,229,222	130,606	25,508	2,427	12,385	2,478	13,123	3,081
Quaking aspen	7,268	3,933	106	68	90	64	15	15
Red alder	151,601	35,108	9,495	2,471	5,256	2,647	4,239	3,525
Sycamore	36,234	36,239	818	818	649	649	169	169
Tanoak	1,556,055	122,019	56,304	4,086	31,862	6,799	24,442	7,757
White alder	42,955	17,817	1,660	884	254	206	1,406	883
Other hardwoods[a]	38,841	29,418	745	293	1,091	482	-346	346
Total	4,034,700	293,667	118,953	8,089	58,118	8,975	60,836	11,201
Total, California	11,887,415	803,728	250,170	14,590	116,995	14,164	133,175	18,131

Note: Gross volume is the volume of a tree from a 1-foot stump to a 4-inch diameter top, with no deduction for cull sections of rot or poor form.

Includes all hardwood trees ≥5 inches diameter at breast height, including sound and rotten cull trees.

Excludes volume from land that transferred to reserved status or national forest ownership in the 1990s.

Excludes volume from land that was converted from forest to developed land, roads, or other types of nonforest in the 1990s.

— = less than 50 cubic feet.

SE = sampling error.

[a] Other hardwoods includes apple, California sycamore, Oregon ash, Pacific dogwood, walnut, water birch, and willow.

Table 16—Total stem volume of hardwood tree mortality between 1984 and 1994, by species and diameter class, on unreserved woodland and timberland, outside national forests, California

| Species | Diameter class (inches at breast height) | | | | | | | | | | | | All classes | |
	1.0-2.9	3.0-4.9	5.0-6.9	7.0-8.9	9.0-10.9	11.0-12.9	13.0-14.9	15.0-16.9	17.0-18.9	19.0-20.9	21.0-28.9	29.0+	Total	SE
	Million cubic feet													
Oak group:														
Blue oak	.7	—	—	—	—	—	—	5.3	—	48.6	33.7	8.3	96.6	45
California black oak	4.8	14.3	11.6	16.3	27.6	6.9	28.0	8.3	14.9	13.5	30.5	47.7	224.4	39
Canyon live oak	3.8	3.7	2.6	.7	2.5	2.0	.1	27.5	61.7	—	12.9	14.5	131.9	90
Coast live oak	—	.3	2.4	9.7	1.1	5.9	2.3	64.0	35.7	—	—	—	121.5	73
Interior live oak	2.7	3.0	2.9	6.2	5.4	—	.1	—	—	—	—	—	20.4	12
Oregon white oak	.5	3.6	2.8	1.4	1.9	.3	—	—	3.7	—	15.4	—	29.7	13
Valley oak	.1	.3	—	—	12.0	2.4	—	—	—	—	27.1	—	41.9	39
Total	12.7	25.2	22.3	34.3	50.5	17.6	30.5	105.1	115.9	62.1	119.7	70.5	666.4	
Non-oak group:														
Bigleaf maple	0.7	1.0	2.5	—	—	.1	.5	—	—	2.1	—	—	6.9	3
Buckeye	1.1	3.7	11.0	10.2	.8	6.4	—	—	—	—	—	—	33.2	18
California laurel	1.1	1.4	7.5	2.4	.1	—	1.2	1.8	2.4	—	.1	2.1	20.1	8
Cottonwood/aspen	—	—	1.0	—	—	.6	—	—	—	—	3.0	—	4.7	4
Eucalyptus	.1	.5	—	—	—	19.4	—	1.4	—	—	—	—	21.4	20
Pacific madrone	3.6	4.9	7.0	9.4	9.7	10.7	14.1	11.3	3.7	1.5	11.9	5.5	93.2	20
Red alder	1.4	4.8	4.8	3.4	.3	1.3	—	.7	1.7	—	—	2.5	20.9	7
Tanoak	9.8	12.3	12.9	9.3	8.6	12.3	6.3	7.6	3.9	4.7	26.1	9.2	122.9	19
White alder	.3	3.2	—	—	—	—	.8	—	—	.7	1.1	—	6.0	4
Other hardwoods[a]	.2	—	—	12.7	—	—	4.5	—	2.4	—	—	—	19.7	19
Total	18.4	31.8	46.7	47.3	19.4	50.8	27.4	22.8	14.0	9.0	42.1	19.3	349.0	
Total, California	31.1	57.0	69.0	81.6	69.9	68.4	57.9	127.9	129.9	71.2	161.8	89.8	1,015.4	165

Note: Total stem volume is the volume of a tree from the ground to the tree tip, with no deductions taken for cull sections.

Includes all hardwood trees ≥1 inch diameter at breast height that were alive in 1981-84 and died during the remeasurement period.

Includes sound and rotten cull trees.

Excludes volume from land that transferred to reserved status or national forest ownership in the 1990s.

Excludes volume from land that was converted from forest to developed land, roads, or other types of nonforest in the 1990s.

— = less than 50,000 cubic feet.

SE = sampling error.

[a] Other hardwoods includes giant chinquapin, Oregon ash, sycamore, Pacific dogwood, and willow.

Table 17—Estimated numbers of large hardwood trees on woodland and timberland, by species and diameter class, California, 1990s

Species	Diameter class (inches at breast height)						All classes	
	11.0-16.9	17.0-22.9	23.0-28.9	29.0-34.9	35.0-40.9	41.0+	Total	SE
	— — — — — — — — — — — — Thousands of trees — — — — — — — — — — — —							%
Oak group:								
Blue oak	32,900	7,400	2,100	400	100	—	42,900	7
California black oak	41,700	11,600	4,100	1,500	500	300	59,700	5
Canyon live oak	39,400	8,400	2,400	900	300	200	51,600	7
Coast live oak	29,200	9,600	2,100	700	300	—	41,900	11
Engelmann oak	500	200	200	100	—	—	1,000	63
Interior live oak	9,900	2,300	300	200	—	—	12,700	13
Oregon white oak	8,400	2,100	500	200	100	—	11,300	15
Valley oak	2,500	700	400	200	100	100	4,000	24
Total	164,500	42,300	12,100	4,200	1,400	600	225,100	
Non-oak group:								
Bigleaf maple	4,500	1,200	200	100	100	—	6,100	15
Black cottonwood	—	—	100	—	—	—	100	53
California buckeye	1,000	—	—	—	—	—	1,000	44
California laurel	6,800	1,100	400	100	—	—	8,400	18
California sycamore	400	100	200	—	—	—	700	47
Eucalyptus	1,300	600	100	—	—	—	2,000	77
Giant chinquapin	1,300	200	100	—	—	—	1,600	23
Oregon ash	200	—	—	—	—	—	200	72
Pacific dogwood	—	—	—	—	—	—	—	77
Pacific madrone	22,800	6,300	2,200	500	200	100	32,100	7
Quaking aspen	1,300	200	—	—	—	—	1,500	42
Red alder	3,400	400	100	—	—	—	3,900	22
Tanoak	39,800	10,100	2,500	600	100	100	53,200	7
White alder	1,400	400	100	—	—	—	1,900	20
Total	84,200	20,600	6,000	1,300	400	200	112,700	
Total, California	248,700	62,900	18,100	5,500	1,800	800	337,000	
SE for total (%)	3	3	4	6	8	11	3	

Note: Excludes reserved lands outside of national forests because these areas were not sampled.

Includes all live hardwood trees ≥11 inches diameter at breast height.

Includes sound and rotten cull trees.

— = less than 500 trees.

SE = sampling error.

Table 18—Estimated numbers of small hardwood trees on woodland and timberland, by species and diameter class, California, 1990s

Species	Seedling	1.0-2.9	3.0-4.9	5.0-6.9	7.0-8.9	9.0-10.9	All classes Total	SE
								%
Oak group:								
Blue oak	247	51	75	66	40	28	507	8
California black oak	698	115	90	70	52	32	1,058	5
Canyon live oak	1,401	308	185	138	80	44	2,158	4
Coast live oak	162	28	15	17	18	12	252	12
Engelmann oak	7	3	4	1	1	—	15	77
Interior live oak	396	197	120	58	26	12	810	10
Oregon white oak	178	39	49	42	23	10	341	12
Valley oak	22	2	3	3	1	2	33	31
Total	3,112	743	541	396	241	142	5,174	
Non-oak group:								
Bigleaf maple	60	31	21	16	9	5	142	10
Black cottonwood	1	—	—	—	—	—	3	51
California buckeye	65	27	11	9	7	3	122	15
California laurel	233	83	37	20	11	6	391	10
California sycamore	5	4	1	1	—	—	10	57
Eucalyptus	5	1	1	—	3	1	11	88
Giant chinquapin	25	10	4	2	2	1	43	19
Oregon ash	11	3	1	—	—	—	15	52
Pacific dogwood	58	48	7	1	—	—	114	13
Pacific madrone	158	80	39	30	21	15	344	8
Quaking aspen	21	11	6	2	1	1	42	32
Red alder	8	34	9	6	6	4	68	23
Tanoak	863	561	205	116	64	38	1,846	4
White alder	11	8	4	2	1	1	26	31
Total	1,525	899	346	206	125	75	3,176	
Total, California	4,637	1,641	886	602	367	217	8,350	
SE for total (%)	3	3	3	4	6	8	3	

Note: Excludes reserved lands outside of national forests because these areas were not sampled.

Includes all live hardwood trees <11 inches diameter at breast height.

Includes sound and rotten cull trees.

— = less than 500,000 trees.

SE = sampling error.

Table 19 — Forest type attributes (area, basal area, and trees per acre) on woodland and timberland, for 12 counties[a] in California quarantined for *Phytophthora ramorum* as of summer 2004

Forest type[c]	Land area				Tree attributes within forest type[b]			
			Privately	Timber-	Average basal area		Average TPA	
	Area	SE	owned	land	Basal area	SE	Trees per acre	SE
	Thousand acres	*%*	*%*	*%*	*Sq. ft. per acre*	*%*	*Number per acre*	*%*
Tanoak	1,031	7	92	100	182	12	256	13
Redwood	690	9	87	100	287	15	250	15
Douglas-fir	642	9	69	100	206	14	191	15
Coast live oak	532	14	81	12	114	21	135	22
Blue oak	444	16	83	1	62	24	93	24
Oregon white oak	299	16	89	42	117	25	186	26
California black oak	244	18	90	67	132	27	169	31
Pacific madrone	223	20	80	79	151	29	184	30
Canyon live oak	209	19	56	58	168	26	251	29
California laurel	163	24	99	58	116	34	153	38
Valley oak	106	35	100	13	66	50	91	51
Interior live oak	56	36	68	33	129	50	138	53
Red alder	48	39	100	100	137	58	214	58
Bigleaf maple	48	39	65	46	111	57	143	57
Mixed conifer	47	28	1	100	228	44	139	40
Other forest types[d]	306	15						
All forest land	5,089	2	81	68	162	5	188	5

Note: Excludes reserved lands outside of national forests because these areas were not sampled.

All data are from inventories conducted in the 1990s.

SE = sampling error.

TPA = trees per acre.

[a] Includes Alameda, Contra Costa, Humboldt, Marin, Mendocino, Monterey, Napa, San Mateo, Santa Clara, Santa Cruz, Solano, and Sonoma Counties.

[b] The average of all live trees (including sound and rotten culls) ≥5 inches diameter at breast height.

[c] Forest types are ordered by the amount of acres present in the 12 counties.

[d] Other forest types include a mixture of hardwood and softwood types; no attributes are presented for this group.

Table 20—Estimated forest land area where host tree species[a] of *Phytophthora ramorum* were present on woodland and timberland, for counties in California quarantined as of summer 2004

County	Forest area for sampled land in 12 counties		Forest area with sudden oak death host trees present[b]		Area of host presence/ forest area
	Area	SE	Area	SE	
	Thousand acres	*%*	*Thousand acres*	*%*	*%*
Alameda	113	35	59	48	52
Contra Costa	52	54	34	66	66
Humboldt	1,615	5	1,478	5	92
Marin	26	73	25	75	97
Mendocino	1,668	5	1,454	6	87
Monterey	551	12	224	16	41
Napa	184	24	87	29	47
San Mateo	59	35	55	35	92
Santa Clara	239	23	162	27	68
Santa Cruz	184	17	180	17	98
Solano	20	68	3	100	18
Sonoma	378	13	354	13	94
Total, California	5,089	2	4,115	3	81

Note: Excludes reserved lands outside of national forests because these areas were not sampled.

All data are from inventories conducted in the 1990s.

SE = sampling error.

[a] Host tree species included: bigleaf maple, California black oak, California buckeye, California laurel, canyon live oak, coast live oak, Douglas-fir, Pacific madrone, redwood, tanoak.

[b] Classification of presence/absence was based on whether a regulated host tree species was present on a subplot of the plot. The estimate of area with host trees present may be underestimated because: (a) understory vegetation and shrubs were not included, (b) seedlings were subsampled on a smaller fixed-radius plot, and (c) trees were sampled with variable-radius sampling.